Crossing Borders

Contemporary Issues in the Middle East

Crossing Borders

An American Woman in the Middle East

☙☙ ☙☙ ☙☙

Judith Caesar

Syracuse University Press

Copyright © 1997 by Syracuse University Press
Syracuse, New York 13244-5160
All Rights Reserved

First Paperback Edition 1999
99 00 01 02 03 04   6 5 4 3 2 1

This book is part of the Mohamed El-Hindi Series on Arab Culture
and Islamic Civilization and is published with the assistance
of a grant from the M.E.H. Foundation.

The paper used in this publication meets the minimum requirements
of American National Standard for Information Sciences—Permanence
of Paper for Printed Library Materials, ANSI Z39.48-1984. ∞™

Library of Congress Cataloging-in-Publication Data
Caesar, Judith.
Crossing borders : an American woman in the Middle East / Judith
Caesar.—1st ed.
p. cm.—(Contemporary issues in the Middle East)
ISBN 0-8156-2735-1 (alk. paper)—ISBN 0-8156-2859-4 (pbk. : alk.paper)
1. Caesar, Judith. 2. Americans—Saudi Arabia—Biography.
3. Americans—Egypt—Biography. 4. Teachers—Saudi Arabia—
Biography. 5. Teachers—Egypt—Biography. 6. Saudi Arabia—Social
life and customs 7. Egypt—Social life and customs. 8. East and
West. I. Title. II. Series.
CT275.C15A3 1997
956'.00413—dc21   97-3686

Manufactured in the United States of America

Contents

Saudi Arabia: 1987–1990

Acknowledgments

I wish first to thank my husband, Mamoun Fandy, for all his help, support, and advice and, second, to thank Dr. Michael Beard, of the University of North Dakota, for reading and commenting on the manuscript so insightfully. But most of all, I want to thank my colleagues, friends, and students in Saudi Arabia and Egypt, who helped me to understand both literature and the world better. I have changed their names and the details of their lives to protect their privacy, but they know who they are, and I thank them.

Judith Caesar was born and raised in western Pennsylvania and received a Ph.D. in American literature from Case Western Reserve University. She taught for five years in Saudi Arabia and was a Senior Fulbright Lecturer in American literature in Egypt. Her articles and book reviews about the Middle East have appeared in the *Christian Science Monitor*, *The Nation*, the *New York Times*, the *Washington Post*, *The Progressive*, and the *Philadelphia Inquirer*. She is also a short story writer, and her fiction has appeared in *The Antioch Review*, *Dalhousie Review*, *Kansas Quarterly*, *Wascana Review*, and *The North American Review*. She currently lives in Arlington, Virginia, with her husband, Mamoun Fandy.

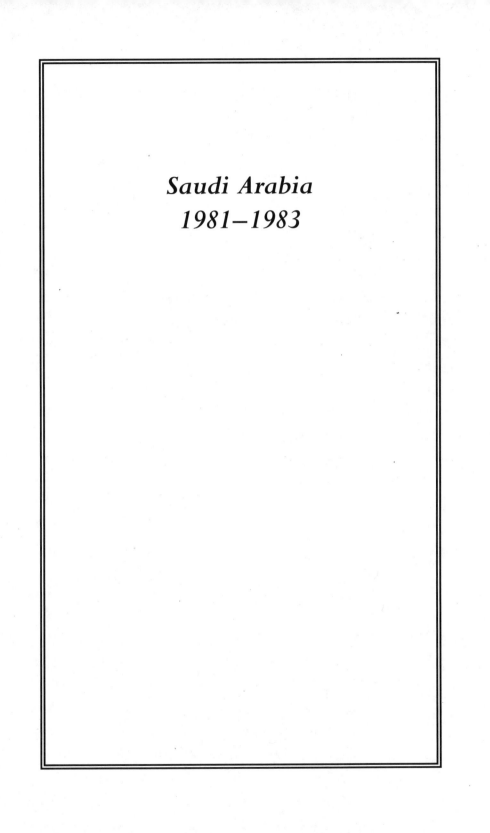

Saudi Arabia
1981–1983

1

Getting Lost, Getting Unlost

Living in another country is like being lost in a strange city. All of the signposts are in a language you can't read. They may even be turned around so the arrows point in the wrong direction. The map issued to you by your society doesn't correspond to where you are. You, a normal, competent adult, are suddenly a child again and no matter what your initial resolve, you begin to resent the culture you have voluntarily come to for making you feel that way.

I arrived in Riyadh in the middle of the night in the middle of August 1981. The man to whom I was married at the time had been awarded a Fulbright grant to teach in Saudi Arabia, and I had been hired as an assistant professor in the women's section of the University of Riyadh's English department. (Later, I was to come back to Saudi Arabia by myself, to get away from the very man I had accompanied there in the first place. But I could guess none of that at the time I first arrived.) Just before the "Fasten seat belt" light flashed on, all the dark-haired and bejeweled women that I had looked at so curiously when I boarded were standing up to wrap black gauze over their faces and *abayahs* (black cloaks) over their bodies. The Saudi man sitting next to me ditched his empty vodka bottle in the stewardess's cart as she hurried past. We were entering a different world.

A wave of heat struck me as I got off the plane. My eyes hurt and I instinctively reached for my sunglasses before I realized that it was the heat and the dryness of the night air that felt like a glare. Dazed with exhaustion already, I moved in a stupor from the plane to the airport and then from the airport out into the heat again. It took an hour to get into the airport building, and another two and one-half hours to get through passport control and customs, a half-dozen flights from other parts of the world having arrived at the same time as mine.

Sitting back in the air-conditioned van driven by I didn't know whom to I didn't know where, I kept seeing after-images of the airport —men in white robes (Saudi), men in baggy trousers and tunics (Pakistanis), men in skirts (Yemenis), men in leisure suits, men in uniforms, Western women in "ordinary" clothes, like me, Sudanese women gracefully draped in yards of flowered chiffon, Saudi women covered in black, Egyptian women with their faces encircled by pastel scarfs. In one night, I'd seen more different nationalities than I had seen before in my whole life and I still didn't know where I was or what it meant for me to be there. In the morning, I told myself, I would wake up and things would be back to normal.

They were not. I was in another country. But I was less exhausted and the sunlight gave me the illusion of normality. I met the other occupants of the guest house, where the recently arrived teachers stayed before being assigned apartments. There was a newly married Iranian couple who had to leave the States for somewhere when their student visas expired—they couldn't return to Iran for political reasons they didn't want to discuss, and an American Ph.D. who hadn't been able to get tenure and his British wife, Rachel, a music teacher who was counting on getting rich by giving Saudi kids violin lessons. (She did not.) None of us knew where we were supposed to go to sign our contracts or apply for housing, and none of us knew anything about Saudi Arabia except what we had read. So we sat around asking each other and making guesses.

To reconnoiter and to buy food for breakfast, the Iranian woman, Faiza, her husband, and I went to look for a grocery store. Although Faiza and I were dressed as modestly as the State Department handbook had told us (skirts below the knee, sleeves below the elbow), we were stared at. Not admiring stares—hostile stares. We had done what the book said. The book lied. I made a note to remember that about books.

"Maybe they want us to wear chadors," Faiza suggested. "And I'm not about to do that."

After we returned, while I was collapsed in the living room of the guest house trying to figure out what had happened, I was joined by Rachel. I don't know what got her started, but she began telling me about her visit to her in-laws in America and about how shallow, ill-mannered, and materialistic Americans were. Her proof was that as soon as she entered an American house, an American host would show her around the house, pointing out his prize possessions: his stereo, his pool, his rec room. "Just to let me know what he had and I didn't," she said. "That's how Americans judge social class. They can't tell by accent, you see, because they all have the same mispronunciations."

Now what exactly was wrong with Rachel's explanation? I suppose we Americans do show guests around our houses, but it had never occurred to me that it was a way of showing off or demonstrating social class. I suspected that it was more often motivated by not knowing what to say or what else to do with relative strangers. Whatever the reason, I was fairly sure it wasn't what Rachel thought it was. I also thought about asking her how 260 million people could be mispronouncing a language but decided I really didn't want to get into an argument just then. For one thing, she knew how to work the bottled gas stove and I didn't.

But I thought, later, about why Rachel had come up with those ideas and what it might have to do with what had just happened to me. Whenever other people do things differently, I decided, we seem to need to explain it. So we fit it into what we have already heard about those people. If we've heard that Americans are ignorant, shallow materialists, or that Arabs are hostile, violent misogynists, we use that to explain the behavior we don't understand. We are so used to connecting understanding the world around us to being fully functional adults that when we are suddenly confronted with a world we don't understand, we tend to latch onto the easiest explanation available. The alternative is to feel stupid and helpless.

There in Saudi Arabia, not knowing the language, not being able to read the street signs (or even the numbers on the apartment doors), not knowing how to work the stove or dispose of the garbage at first, and, later, totally missing social signals, I certainly felt stupid and helpless, and I hated it. In America, not knowing what was implied what must have driven Rachel slightly crazy too, if she weren't always that way. That was perhaps why she was so happy with her stereotype. And of course the "they're awful, those people" explanation has the added virtue of eliminating the need to examine the society in more detail. If they're that awful, why bother? But I should have kept in mind that it is a crazy person's response, or at least the response of someone experiencing the temporary insanity of culture shock.

Having figured that out about stereotypes of Americans (and I have encountered many Europeans with that attitude), I should have immediately applied it to the stereotypes I had of Arabs. Later, however, when American expatriates told me that Arabs hated women and that they were narrow minded and irrationally violent, I believed them. Some of the stories they told about Saudi society were enough to terrify me into reduced sanity. Not only was it against the law for women to drive cars, I was told, but a woman could be arrested for simply being in a car with a man not her husband. In fact, the Morality Police, the *mutawas* (later I learned the correct plural was *mutawaeen*) had the power to arrest anyone, and once arrested, you had no rights. Mail was censored and phone calls monitored. Foreign women rumored to be having love affairs could be thrown out of the country, with their passports stamped "Prostitute." Every year, some Westerner would have a nervous breakdown.

All this information was related to me by an American who had been teaching at the university for several years; in fact, he told it with such glee that it crossed my mind that the horrors he described gave him a kind of pleasure. The stories were echoed, in almost the same tone, by many other Western men to whom I spoke. Hearing these stories from so many different people and seeing enough to lend some credibility to the rumors (the *mutawaeen* glowering and rapping their walking sticks against the windows of shops late in closing for prayers, for instance), I was quite ready to believe, I'm sorry to say, that Arabs were the incarnation of everything horrible.

I might have gone on thinking that way if I hadn't become friends with Arab women whose values contradicted what I had been told and who gave me alternative explanations. They were not, I concluded, simply being defensive. Some of what the Western men had told me was apparently quite true—or at least the Arab women thought so. They told me that Saudi Arabia was indeed a police state and gave me horrifying examples of their own. They talked to me about the very real problems they faced as educated women in a traditional society like Saudi Arabia. But I learned from them that not all Arab societies are like Saudi society. I met Egyptian and Jordanian women who drove cars and went around unveiled in their own countries, women who were respected for their education both at home and in Saudi Arabia. I also figured out, at last, that there is a big difference between what governments do and what most of their people think is right. Despite my own anger at the failure of American policies to live up to what I took to be American ideals, I somehow had never thought that Arabs might feel the same mixture of love and anger toward their countries as well—or might be as sensitive to criticisms from foreigners. I learned, for instance, that many Saudis (and almost all non-Saudi Arabs) were even more afraid of the *muta-*

waeen than Westerners were, and for good reason. If they were arrested, they couldn't just call to their embassy to get out of the country, for instance.

I came to realize that blaming "the Arabs," was not the answer. I suppose a lot of other American expatriates didn't understand this partly because they didn't have the chance, as I did, to get to know Arab people through a common interest in literature, or indeed in anything else. And they also had to hold the same notions as the other expats to get along with them—the same phenomenon that Forster describes among the British Raj in *A Passage to India*. I was lucky enough to find friends outside the expat cliques.

No matter how open minded I tried to be, however, I still made mistakes. I experienced the phenomenon, for instance, of what I came to think of as the false cultural cognate—I would see something in Arab society that resembled something in American society and assume the same motivation behind it. In a way, this is the opposite of "they're awful, those people." It's a variation of "they're really just like us," which is wrong too.

When I first started teaching some weeks later, for instance, I had an extremely puzzling experience. The students seemed lively and friendly; there was no mistaking their pleasant smiles for hostility. How then could I explain the fact that as I was lecturing, they would suddenly bunch their upturned fingers together and wave them at me in what looked like a very rude gesture? Of course, I thought it odd that even the most hostile student would be so foolhardy as make rude gestures at me in class. Nevertheless, puzzled and at least somewhat offended, I assumed a stern expression to let them know I wasn't going to put up with any nonsense and tried to finish the lecture as quickly as possible to get away from them.

It wasn't until I was sitting in my office with an Arab colleague that I learned what the gesture meant. While we were talking, a student appeared in the doorway to talk to one of us; the teacher bunched her fingers at the girl, not even interrupting the conversation, and the girl went away.

"What did you just do?" I asked.

She seemed surprised. "Oh, I just told her to wait a minute."

I then asked her why my students were doing that in class. And of course they were trying to signal to me that I was talking too fast for them to take notes. They wanted me to slow down, wait a minute, and probably wondered why I was ignoring them. Not entirely convinced, I decided to try the gesture myself and see what happened. I carefully picked occasions when a rude gesture would have expressed my reactions, just in case my colleague was wrong: when I couldn't cross the street at a crosswalk because none of the cars would slow down, for instance, or when I couldn't think straight because all my students were crowding around my desk shouting questions at once. Somewhat to my surprise, no one looked offended. In fact, cars stopped to let me cross and students stopped crowding and instead waited their turns. Yet at the end of the year I still heard Americans declare it was an obscene gesture and use it as proof of the crudeness of Arabs. It made me wonder how many comparable mistakes I had made about larger issues.

For one thing, like most Westerners, I had gotten veils wrong. I remember reading a *National Geographic* article about Sudan, in which the writer said that Sudanese women covered their heads as a sign of their inferiority. It is not an illogical assumption. Because Christian women have traditionally covered their heads in church as a mark of respect, it is easy to assume that an Arab Muslim woman's covering her head in front of a man indicates the same deference.

Thus, my first reaction to seeing women swathed in black from head to foot was absolute horror. This response persisted until the Saudi student who lived across the street from me offered me a regular ride to work in her chauffeur-driven car. She swept down the stairs of her apartment building, a blur of black, and the driver jumped out of the car to open the door for her. She kept up a running conversation with him as we drove to school, sometimes laughing, sometimes scolding. She even had him stop at the newsstand every morning and pick up a newspaper for each of us. (She read hers through her veil.) She was one of the most self-possessed—and self-confident—young women I had encountered anywhere. And after seeing fully veiled women yelling at shopkeepers they thought were cheating them, or talking back to the *mutawaeen* who tried to bustle them out of shops for prayers before they were ready to leave, I decided it was time to revise my opinion about what veils meant.

So I asked the girl how she felt to be wearing all that black so that no one could see what she looked like, especially as she was sitting next to an apparently emancipated American woman with uncovered hair and no *abayah*.

"Safe," she said. "I feel safe." And then she added, "I think until there is no such thing as sexual harassment in this world, men don't deserve to be able to look at women."

So much for inferiority.

How did she feel about the way I was dressed? "Why should you wear a veil? It's not your custom. If wearing a veil makes you feel like you're living in a box, don't do it. But of course men will stare."

Ah, I told myself. If being in another culture is like being lost, then the way to get unlost is to do exactly what any sensible person would: admit to being lost and ask directions of someone who looks like she might live around there. Why doesn't everyone do that?

Of course, I knew some of the answers. Some people will always insist that they know the way and end up getting more and more lost, frustrated, and furious when the outside world refuses to comply with their sense of where they are. They lose their heads. They lose themselves. Although it is too glib to say that sometime in 1981, I found myself in Saudi Arabia, at least I can say that by asking questions, I gradually became sufficiently unlost to begin to see where I was.

2

Souk

Soon after I arrived in Riyadh and moved into an apartment on Khaz-zan Street, I learned that I could alleviate my boredom and disorienta-tion by means other than standing on the dusty balcony of my apartment building looking out at the dustier street. I could walk down to the Dira Souk. My Arab neighbors had assured me that it was "too far to walk," but I soon discovered that it was only too far to walk for a woman in spike heels trying to keep her *abayah* closed to the desert wind with one hand while clutching her purse in the other. For someone wearing running shoes and a backpack, the only problem was crossing a four-lane highway, for which one only needed a certain amount of fatalism.

At first I went with the other Americans in my building because, in the midst of such foreignness, I wanted to be surrounded by people as much like me as I could find. It took me three or four such excur-sions to decide that perhaps they really were not as much like me as I had supposed. Furthermore, as the group was composed of both men and women, we were about as inconspicuous as a parade.

It was through these other Americans, however, that I encountered the American teacher (I think his name was Bill) whose story became such a disturbing part of my first year in Saudi Arabia. We stopped by primarily because Bill lived in a building near the souk and we were all tired and thirsty.

Bill was unlike any American I had previously met there. Al-though he too had just arrived in the country, he came to the door in the plaid wrap-around skirtlike garment worn by Yemeni men, something other Western men would only wear at the embassy Hal-loween party. Like the Arabs I had met, he thrust cold soft drinks into our hands before we got a chance to sit down. And unlike almost any other Western man I knew, he liked Saudi Arabia.

It was clear at a glance that Bill had had bad luck in the apartments assigned to us by the university housing department. The brown velveteen overstuffed living room suite was just like the one in my own apartment, but it was much older. The building was far more run down as well, and I suspected it of harboring even more cockroaches.

The American professor who was playing "old hand" in guiding us through the souk immediately told Bill to demand better housing.

"If you let them take advantage of you like this, they won't respect you," he told him.

"I don't know," Bill replied. "I kind of like it here. It gives me more chance to meet people."

Then Bill went on to talk about the various Third World "guest workers" he had met in the park across the street, how he had exchanged English lessons for Arabic lessons with an Egyptian waiter, and how the building's Yemeni janitor had invited him for tea.

As we left, the old hand muttered, "This guy isn't going to make it if he's going native already."

At home, thinking of Bill and the old hand, I wrote in my journal, "Americans abroad either become more American or less so. If we become more so, we get obnoxious, and if we become less so, we get weird."

I can never remember any conscious decision to become less American (or weird) myself. I simply drifted into it. My Egyptian neighbor across the hall, Zainab, who had just gotten her Ph.D. from the University of Iowa, shared my interest in feminist readings of literature. I started going to the souk with her or with her teenage daughter, Reem, who spoke no more English than I had learned of Arabic but who was more eager than her mother to put on a pair of sneakers and walk the three-quarters of a mile to the Dira Souk.

Suddenly I no longer felt like a majorette. At first I didn't understand my relative invisibility. I still wore my hair uncovered, and although I wore a long skirt, I didn't wear an *abayah*. Reem, in an *abayah* and *turha* (headscarf) but with her face uncovered, would have blended in with the other Arab girls if she hadn't worn sneakers and insisted on carrying her mother's U of Iowa backpack. I finally decided that I was inconspicuous because I was with an Arab girl. Arab women, I began to observe, seemed to go shopping in pairs or groups. Apparently, onlookers were no longer wondering which of the men with me was my boyfriend and if I were looking for an additional one.

Feeling more at ease, I was less troubled by the differentness of shopping in a souk, particularly the crowding that so unnerved me when I felt surrounded by foreigners. I never really liked the fact that a dozen people were crowded together in a shop the size of a kitchen, but it wasn't frightening when I realized that most of these people were other women and that none were much different from the students I saw every day in my classes. It didn't even bother me that other women would take me by the shoulders, whisper *"lau samahti"* and gently push me out of the way, especially after I learned that this only meant "excuse me" and realized that by lingering in a doorway I was blocking traffic. In fact, the proximity of so many people seemed reassuring.

It was still exotic that the shopkeepers were not only Saudi but Pakistani, Egyptian, Turkish, and Yemeni, and that the goods came from all over the world: electrical equipment from Taiwan, clothing from India and Egypt, incense from Yemen, and silver and amber jewelry from the local Bedouin women, who roamed around the souk with half-veils revealing eyes made up with kohl. The shoppers, poor and middle-class Saudis, Filipina hospital workers, Korean construction workers, Yemenis, and Sudanese, all mixed without any apparent ethnic tensions. And although the buildings of Riyadh all seemed to be the same dusty beige, the shops had their wares hanging on floor-to-ceiling racks in the front: *gellabeyahs* (Egyptian robes) of all colors, children's toys, Oriental carpets. Here was diversity in all things.

This gave the souk a feeling entirely different from the rest of the city. It was life and color. Because of this, I didn't even mind getting lost in the souk, which seemed at first a maze of winding alleyways, narrow so that the surrounding buildings would always cast shade on the shoppers. I soon learned that each type of goods was sold in a separate section of the souk, so that we could begin to determine where we were by what was being sold. Some day, I told myself, I would find my way around the society and culture in the same way.

Instead, I always remained more of a spectator. On a literal level, I never got used to bargaining for everything, perhaps because I wasn't any good at it and could seldom get more than a couple of riyals (about seventy cents) off the original price. And yet I enjoyed watching Zainab and Reem in action—the sudden coy smiles; the protestations of having only a few riyals with them; their lack of embarrassment at having the shopkeeper show almost everything in the store to them, only for them to shake their heads dubiously and walk away (slowly, to give the merchant time to run after them offering a better price). I also noted the way young Saudi women would raise their face veils, ostensibly to see the color of the merchandise better, but in fact to give the merchant a smile he might consider worth a discount or at least a compliment. The only time I ever got a bargain was when I discovered I had left my wallet at home and only had the money in my pocket, a ploy I felt uncomfortable about contriving.

At dusk, when the shops closed for prayers, Reem and I would buy sodas from one of the women vendors who sat in the corners of the souk with washtubs full of ice water and cold (or at least cool) soft drinks. Women, who are not normally allowed in mosques (although they are in many other Muslim countries), would wait outside in the alleys or in cars until the shops would reopen about twenty minutes later. Reem and I would sit on the curb, drinking our sodas and watching the sunset. The dust in the air and the cloudless skies made every sunset spectacular, and I came to think, as I watched the crowds thin out and felt the beginning of the evening breeze, that moments like these were ones I would miss when I left Saudi Arabia.

When the sunset prayer was over, Reem and I would go back to our shopping, which consisted mostly of looking and debating about whether the items before us were *helwa* (cute) or *wehisha* (ugly). The most garish purple taffetas and silver lamés invariably struck Reem as *helwa*, whereas everything that I found tasteful she declared *wehisha*, frequently accompanying her remarks with gagging noises in case I had missed her point. Despite this, we got along well, which made me wonder if these were the only two words one really needed to know to communicate with any thirteen-year-old girl.

The souk itself was shades of meaning. By evening, the *shuwarmah* stands would open, filling the air with the scent of garlic and lemon and chicken. Watching the Lebanese *shuwarmah* makers whittling the meat off the rotisseries, mixing it with parsley and tomatoes, and wrapping it in pita bread, all with great flourishes of carving knives, was like watching Japanese chefs, except that the show was conducted on the street for anybody to watch. Sometimes we would buy *shuwar-mah* sandwiches to take back with us, the grease from the meat inevitably soaking through the bag by the time we got back.

In the evening, I decided, Riyadh suddenly became a livable city, as the darkness covered the building rubble, and the empty streets that made Riyadh look like a ghost town during the day filled with people. If I didn't feel at home, I did feel more comfortable being out of place and perhaps closer to questioning if I did truly have a place anywhere.

Yet even then, flush with new confidence and still excited by being is such a strange new place, I saw evidence of a more complex world, which should have alerted me to another layer of reality beneath the exoticism. The carpet section of the souk, I learned, was called "the Afghan souk" because most of the merchants were Afghani refugees, quiet, stocky men with high cheekbones and slightly Oriental eyes. They were different from the other merchants in manner as well, slightly more formal, almost withdrawn. Looking at the carpets, I found it only odd and somewhat kitschy that the stylized flowers and trees of traditional Afghan and Persian designs would suddenly give way to equally stylized tanks and Kalishnakovs woven into the soft maroons and indigos of the carpets. Later, it seemed like a metaphor for what had happened to a whole society. I didn't know it then, but most of the Third World foreigners were refugees from some cold war political and economic disaster: Filipinos from the collapsing Marcos Regime, and Sri Lankans, Sudanese, and Lebanese from civil war. But at the time, none of this seemed to have anything to do with me.

I thought of the souk later as the essence of what Saudi Arabia could have been, had times and governments been kinder. Although the "old hand" had expressed the need for distance (not going native) and power ("they won't respect you if . . .") in dealing with Arabs, the world of the souk thrived on proximity and negotiation. The exterior of Saudi Arabia suggested uniformity and artificially clear distinctions: beige buildings, black cloaked women and white-robed men, everyone carefully categorized as Saudi, Western, or Third World National. Saudis even gave the same carefully worded responses to the questions of strangers about politics and religion. The souk was color, pluralism, and tolerance—the same traits I found when I got past the exteriors of houses and relationships. I was always a guest there, just as I was usually just a sightseer in the souk, but what I saw was as real as the shops and the alleyways.

Yet if the souk was one layer of reality beneath the barren exterior, a different, harsher reality also underlay the world of the souk. For one thing, I found out that the square next to the souk was where the Saudi government performed some of its public beheadings. And four months after I met Bill, the American teacher who had gone native, I heard that he had been arrested in the park across from his building for homosexuality, along with a young Indonesian. I learned few of the particulars of the arrest; indeed, all I heard were second-and third-hand rumors. Apparently he confessed after a day or two in custody, which made it "impossible" for either socially well-placed Saudi students or American consular officials to intervene on his behalf. He was in prison for four months and received one hundred lashes before being deported. Later, when I read in the report of the Minnesota Lawyers International Human Rights Committee on Saudi Arabia* that torture is often used to extract confessions, I wondered if Bill's confession had been forced by torture. I was even more disturbed when I read *Human Rights Watch World Report 1993* and learned that the United States government had ignored the case of another American, Scott Nelson, who wanted to sue the Saudi government for having tortured him (337). In light of all of the later publicity about the Michael Fay case in Singapore, I could not help wondering if some sort of unpleasant bargain had been struck between the two governments concerning American silence toward Saudi human rights abuses.

But at the time, I knew none of this, and in the souk, the bargains struck were almost unfailingly honest. Both parties knew what was being sold, and for how much, and the items exchanged were all material. The winding streets created a natural cooling shade, and in the evening dusk, everything ugly vanished with the sunlight. The lighted shops revealed only excited crowds of shoppers from all over the world.

* Minnesota Lawyers International Human Rights Committee, *Shame in the House of Saud: Contempt for Human Rights in Saudi Arabia* (Minneapolis, 1991).

3

All the News That's Fit to Print

When I first went to Saudi Arabia, I had no particular interest in politics. During the Vietnam War, I had been more concerned with the erosion of freedom of expression in America than I was with events in Southeast Asia. For one thing, I knew I didn't know a thing about Southeast Asia, but I had read the Bill of Rights. I was even less concerned with the 1967 Arab-Israeli War; that was just something else that happened during the Vietnam War. In 1973, I was working on my dissertation and listening to news about Watergate. Events in the Middle East seemed far away.

Of course, inspired by the movie, I had read *Exodus* when I was in high school, which made it very clear who the good guys and the bad guys were. However, after seeing *Lawrence of Arabia*, I had also read *The Seven Pillars of Wisdom*, which gave a rather different view of Arabs and which, even as a teenager, I realized was a better book. On a less literary level, it was still pretty much a toss-up between Paul Newman and Omar Sharif.

In Saudi Arabia, I met people who cared passionately about politics, for reasons I could begin to understand if not fully absorb. Rasheed, for example, was an affable eighteen-year-old Palestinian boy who had shown my husband and me around the neighborhood and was always a willing interpreter. He told me that his grandparents had been killed in 1947 because they had refused to leave their house and that all his uncles and cousins had died in refugee camps in Lebanon and Jordan.

Although I heard it, I couldn't really feel it. I couldn't connect that kind of tragic past to a friendly, chubby boy with glasses and horrible blue jeans designed somewhere in the Third World where the theory ruled that the more rivets, pockets, and zippers a pair of jeans had, the classier they were. He was about to go away to the American Univer-

16

sity in Cairo, which seemed appropriate, because as far as I could tell, his most immediate goal was to turn himself into an imitation American.

And indeed most of his relatives had died before he was born. He had only their stories. He himself had never been outside of Saudi Arabia. I didn't know then about the precarious position of Palestinians in Saudi Arabia and everywhere else in the Arab world, because he seldom talked about it. He was too excited about leaving. And so his stories about his family seemed as remote and as surreptitiously exciting as the images of violence that flash across the TV screen, as you sit at home knowing that everyone you care about is so safe that their safety never enters your consciousness. Rasheed looked safe— safer, in fact, than a lot of the kids I had known in college who smoked pot and muttered about revolution.

Zainab, my Egyptian colleague and neighbor, was another story. She was not an imitation anything. She wore embroidered and appliqued *gellebeyahs* and could speak with equal authority on George Meredith's heroines and Sadat's economic policies. The former, she told me, surpassed Henry James in his understanding of women, and the latter surpassed Hoover in his devastation of a country's economy. Conditionally, I took her word for it, because I knew something about the skills of the two Americans but little about the others. We consumed cup after cup of Turkish coffee (which I had not yet developed a taste for but still preferred to her undrinkable "American" coffee) while she explained how Sadat had given the entrepreneurial class carte blanche to loot the country.

One time, she said, onions had virtually disappeared from the Egyptian markets—bought up by entrepreneurs and exported to Europe. "And this is the staple food of the poor—they eat mostly bread and beans and rely on the onions to give it at least some flavor."

I sipped and listened and reserved judgment. I was used to hearing American academics talk about Reagan in similar terms and figured that I was not going to learn whether they were right or not without reading more of the verbose prose of social scientists than I was willing to subject myself to. But I liked Zainab for caring if the poor could afford onions, whether Sadat was culpable or not.

It was much easier to see that things were very wrong in Saudi Arabia than to contemplate what might be wrong in Egypt. I could tell things were wrong when the English language news magazines had pages ripped out of them; when the Egyptian and Lebanese newspapers wouldn't arrive, to the disappointment of the student with whom I rode to school; or when a Saudi student referred to the Ministry of Information as the Ministry of Denial. "We know something bad and probably true has been written about Saudi Arabia whenever the Ministry of Information tells us to ignore the lies we have heard," she explained. But all of this was accepted with such patient mockery that I began to perceive it as almost normal myself.

Then two things happened that disturbed the balance I was trying so hard to maintain. One evening, when I stopped over to visit Zainab, I found a young Saudi couple with her, very quiet, very formally polite. The man was small-boned, had a faint moustache, and looked at the coffee table rather than at me when he talked. His wife had big brown eyes and a nervous manner, which made her look like a frightened deer. Making stilted conversation with them while Zainab was in the kitchen, I learned that they were from Mecca and that the woman, Amal, was a former student of Zainab's who was about to leave for the States to do graduate work. Her husband, Ahmed, was going with her even though he already had his degree, because under Saudi law Amal could not leave the country without being accompanied by her husband or father. Getting into graduate school in the United States had been difficult, she told me, because she came from a minor tribe and thus could not get a Saudi government scholarship. Because of her grades and recommendations, however, she had been accepted at the University of Colorado and offered a partial scholarship.

The conversation flagged. Ahmed fidgeted with a string of prayer beads and sighed. Apparently it was still somewhat uncertain if they would actually go, and they didn't want to talk about it.

I racked my brain for questions about Mecca, but the only thing I could think to ask was if they had been there two years before when fundamentalists had taken over the Grand Mosque.

"It wasn't fundamentalists," Ahmed said quietly.

When I looked surprised, he went on. "I know you didn't get the story in America—everyone just believed what the government said."

When Zainab came back with a tray of coffee, Amal gave her a worried look. Zainab said something in Arabic, and Amal smiled, but the smile still looked nervous.

"Zainab was telling us that it was safe to tell you these things," she said.

And the story they told was indeed remarkable. Ahmed said that the 1979 incident had been part of a coordinated effort to overthrow the monarchy and replace it with a more democratic government. Leftists, dissident tribesmen, Shiites, and religious leaders were all working together. The Islamists who were part of the plot were not against "modernization," as had been reported, but rather against the rule of the Saud family, which they claimed was corrupt, unjust, and dictatorial. Johaiman al-Otaibi, the leader of the protesters, was from a tribe that had always resisted the Sauds, and the rebellion was perhaps as much tribal as it was religious. The Sauds never had influence beyond Dirri'ia and Riyadh; the rest of the country was dominated by other tribes. The Sauds would have never been able to seize control of the Hejaz (western Saudi Arabia) from the Hashemites back in the 1920s without British help, they told me.

He also told me that the takeover of the mosque was peaceful —the protestors included women and children—and that the Saudi government had sent in American troops to kill them. Both Western and Arab newspapers knew about what happened because sympathizers had notified them.

"Nobody dared to print what really happened," Ahmed told me.

This sounded too strange to be true. It didn't make sense to me, for one thing, that the Saudi government could send in American troops.

"They were afraid to send Saudis. They were afraid their own soldiers wouldn't fire on women and children in a mosque. Maybe the soldiers weren't Americans, but they were Western. I guessed American because there are so many American soldiers here."

"I don't think there are American soldiers here," I said. "I'm sure I've never heard of American soldiers being sent here."

"They keep it very quiet," he told me. Ten years later, in the days leading up to the 1990 Gulf War, Prince Bandar took the CBS *60 Minutes* crew on a tour of American military bases all across Saudi Arabia. Apparently, Ahmed knew what he was talking about. I also checked what he said about the history of the Saud family. He seems to have been right about that as well.

At the time, though, it was too much paranoia for me, and I didn't know how I could ask him how he knew these things without convincing him that I was a spy. We drifted back to the difficulties of graduate work in the States.

I did ask Zainab about it later. "I wasn't in Mecca at the time myself," she told me, "but they were. And I know they are not liars."

Of course, people can repeat rumors without being liars, and that was what I assumed to be the case with Ahmed and Amal. To be fair to them, though, what else could people do but repeat rumors when their press was censored? Everybody in Saudi Arabia repeated rumors, including the Western expatriates, although the rumors of the latter generally concerned xenophobic attacks on Westerners and, as far as I could tell, served primarily as a way of hazing newcomers.

A few days later, Zainab came to my door looking very shaken. "I've just heard the news," she said. "Will you come down to the newsstand with me to see if they have the Egyptian papers?"

I didn't know what she was talking about, but I was always glad to get out of the apartment and I was very curious. We caught a taxi driven by a white-bearded man who blasted Bedouin music out of the tape deck. Zainab was chewing her lower lip so intently that she had most of the frosted pink lipstick off by the time we reached the newsstand.

"Sadat has just arrested over a thousand of Egypt's top intellectuals last night. Virtually everybody who has ever written a word against him. I've been trying to get a call through to Egypt all morning, and I can't get a line. Everything's busy. Or they aren't letting calls through."

She told the driver to wait and dashed into the newsstand. The papers were all sold out. She threw her hands up and looked as if she would have torn her hair if she hadn't had a scarf over it. This sudden avid interest in current events was a side of Zainab I hadn't seen before, and I couldn't quite figure it out at first. I think now that if I had not been so accustomed to disassociating events on the news from events in real life, I might not have been so naïve about the whole thing.

I later learned that Zainab's brother was a prominent member of an opposition party, many of whose members had been arrested, and that the newspaper Zainab had been looking for so frantically was *Al-Ahram*, which had published the names of all those arrested. I later saw the paper and the list.

If it was all too much to absorb and think about at the time, there was plenty of time later and more than enough events and conversations to keep me from forgetting.

About a month later, I took a short vacation to Greece. It was the time of the Haj pilgrimage and the Adha festival that followed it, and schools were closed throughout Saudi Arabia. In Greece, I thought, I could get away to a different world, and in many ways I did. There were beaches and sidewalk cafés and retsina. But there were also women dressed all in black, old men with grizzled moustaches sitting in coffee houses playing backgammon and dominoes, and young girls carefully chaperoned by mothers or aunts—a world not so different from the one across the Mediterranean in Egypt, just somewhat less poor.

The big difference was that in Greece there were elections. Almost ten years before, the Greeks had gotten rid of the military junta that ruled them—or rather, the junta had stepped down after the Cyprus episode—and I never saw any people as excited about elections as the Greeks were. In every town square in Crete, loudspeakers were booming the appeals of the candidates, every piece of wall not an ancient ruin was covered with election posters, and every evening the streets were filled with banner-waving demonstrators.

Crossing Syntagma Square in Athens on my way to a nightclub, I suddenly found myself in the midst of a socialist party rally. I am not good at estimating crowd size, but I can't be too far off in saying that there were thousands of people in the square, most of them cheering or singing or waving banners. I hadn't seen an English language newspaper in a week, but I surmised from the mood of the crowd that the socialists must have had won. I really didn't want to join them, however. Although this was all very nice for them, what I wanted to do was go to a nightclub, but I couldn't move because of all the people around me. After almost an hour, I finally extricated myself and tried to find my way back to the hotel through side streets. Abandoning the idea of a nightclub, I finally settled for an ouzo and a cup of Greek coffee (the same stuff Zainab called Turkish coffee) in a café next to the hotel. In the warm, starry night, vine leaves rustling overhead in the evening breeze, I could still hear the crowd in the distance, and at last I had a moment to sort through my thoughts. The one that kept recurring was that Egyptians and Saudis both would have been jailed or killed for doing what the Greeks were doing that night and indeed for what they had been doing for the past weeks: putting up posters, handing out leaflets, and holding public rallies for a nongovernment party. And the difference was by no means entirely a difference in culture. It was much more an accident of history.

Then as I picked up my room key, the concierge asked me if I had heard the news.

"That the socialists won?"

"That Sadat has been killed."

The next day, I searched out a newsstand and bought an international *Newsweek,* but it didn't tell me much about what had just happened. I skimmed the article for the main points: Islamic extremists, strangely little public mourning, Cairo quiet—then long eulogies about Sadat the statesman.

More telling pieces of information came later. Several months after that, visiting Cairo, I talked to Rasheed about it. For a week after the assassination, he had been afraid to leave his dorm room at American University in Cairo because the police were arresting all the Palestinians they could find. Only when it became reasonably clear that the assassination was not a Palestinian plot did he feel safe enough to go out and place a call to his family to let them know he was all right. An Egyptian to whom I spoke, a graduate student at Assyut University, told me about being arrested along with hundreds of other college students who had demonstrated in favor of having elections rather than Hosni Mubarak's automatically assuming power. The *Newsweek* article did not mention either the mass arrests of Palestinians or the student democracy demonstrations.

When I returned to the United States the following summer, I discovered that the American media had not reported the mass arrests of Egyptian intellectuals before the assassination. In fact, when I mentioned it, people looked at me as if I'd been out in the sun too long over there. I began to wonder if I had hallucinated seeing that newspaper, or if all the Egyptians who told me about it were liars; the alternative was to believe that American news media were censored, at least after a fashion. A thousand arrests in a single night, reported in a newspaper with a circulation of over one million—how could an event like this disappear without a trace? I had seen the newspaper myself, after I had learned enough Arabic to sound out the names, even though I couldn't read the rest of the article. Yet I never saw any mention of the arrests in print until almost ten years later, when I came across a reference to it in a scholarly journal.

My sense of understanding the world cracked a little further at the end of the academic year, when we were all preparing to go home for the summer. The Western teachers were all besieging the Saudia Airline office, trying to exchange their Riyadh-to-New York tickets for ones with stopovers in Europe. Zainab's dowdy and grumpy Lebanese friend, Aziza, had a very different problem. I didn't follow her problem very closely at first, because I didn't particularly like her and because her fears seemed so improbable. Married to an Englishman who stayed in London, she supported the family with her teaching job in Riyadh and took care of their two-year-old daughter. She seemed to spend most of her time complaining—about the students, about Saudi Arabia, about American foreign policy, about everything except what she seemed to me to have cause to complain about, her husband. Now, at the end of the school year, she claimed that the Israelis were about to invade Lebanon and that she needed a stopover in Beirut so that she could take her elderly mother back to England with her. Because I couldn't think of any reason for the Israelis to invade Lebanon, I didn't pay any more attention to this than I did to her assertions that her students hated her because she was a Christian or that America was just like the Roman Empire.

Then one evening when she and Zainab and I were watching the news on Zainab's television, we saw Israeli tanks rolling into a Lebanese village. "I know that village," Aziza screamed, jumping to her feet. "My aunt lives there." Zainab put her arm around Aziza's shoulders. The three of us gazed in horror at the people running for cover, at houses exploding. One of those old women running down the street dodging bullets could have been Aziza's aunt.

Aziza was allowed her stopover in Beirut, but by the time she had the ticket, the Beirut airport was closed. Since Aziza didn't go back to teaching in Riyadh the following year, I never learned if her mother survived the siege of Beirut. Something changed in me after that. Even now, when I look at images of civilians dodging bullets in Sarajevo or Gaza, I think, "Somebody's aunt. Somebody's mother. Somebody's grandson."

And I wonder still if Ahmed and Amal had been right after all in everything that they said, everything that I dismissed at the time, everything that fit into such a seductively conspiratorial pattern later. How could I ever know for sure? I began to wonder what I could ever be certain of, unless I had seen it with my own eyes, and then I realized I couldn't believe that entirely either. If I had watched the invasion of Lebanon in the States, without that year in Saudi Arabia, without Zainab and Aziza standing beside me, I would not have seen the women who might have been Aziza's aunt. I would only have seen a bunch of faceless Arabs.

Perhaps I was naïve not to suspect that American newspapers were less than thorough about reporting the undemocratic practices of American allies. I was also naïve to assume that the events on the international news were not happening to people like the ones I knew. The problem was that I met very few Americans who didn't share that naïveté. Americans might be suspicious of slanted or incomplete coverage of domestic events, but most people I talked to seemed to assume that international coverage was more or less accurate. Indeed, one of the difficult things for me about going back to the States was having so many former friends disbelieve what I told them about the Middle East. They also didn't want to hear about Zainab or Rasheed or any of the other educated and articulate women and men I came to know. It was just too different—and it called for too many imaginative adjustments. To believe me was to question everything they had read, and thus to be in the same quandary that I was. It was too much to ask.

4

Veils Beyond Veils

Outside the walls of the women's campus was the usual morning chaos. Between fifty and one hundred beeping cars crowded around a single gate, each driver determined that his passenger would be exposed to the outside world for no more than a few feet. The students, veiled head to ankle in identical *abayahs,* were getting out of their chauffeur-or dad-driven cars to start another day at the college.

Once the students arrived inside the walls, flipped up their face veils, and headed for class, removing their *abayahs* as they walked, a whole new set of rules applied. Imagination and self-expression replaced anonymity. Although the students were required to wear ankle-length green skirts, they could wear whatever blouses they chose. This in itself required a certain sartorial inventiveness, as most of the colors flattering to olive-skinned brunettes clashed with the green skirts. They could wear tasteful white or beige blouses and look like grown-up girl scouts. They could opt for reds and purples and look radiant but garish. And a few could find blouses in the narrow range of rose and lavender that went with both skirt and complexion. I always admired those girls.

Sometimes they wore T-shirts with slogans on them. One student always came to her first class in a shirt that said, "World's Greatest Student," which impressed ever-hopeful teachers. Others slogans were nationalistic: "Free Palestine," "Visit Egypt" (the latter seemed more feasible), or "Sunny Saudi." But the one that interested me the most was, "I May Not Be Perfect but Parts of Me Are Excellent." I suspect she knew exactly what she was implying.

Most students favored stiletto-heeled sandals that I called the bikinis of the feet. Because their feet were the only parts of their bodies to show in public, this was a way of signaling their youth and feminine attractiveness to interested young men. These shoes were hardly practical at school, however, because the buildings were some distance apart. Worse, since new water and sewer lines were being installed to many of the buildings, the students frequently had to jump over open ditches to get to class. This is no mean feat for a woman in spike heels and an ankle-length skirt. Apparently, however, this developed athletic skills among the students. The only women to fall were two middle-aged professors, an American and an Egyptian, who ended up with a broken arm and a sprained ankle, respectively. I often thought that if the high-heeled ditch jump were to become an Olympic event, the Saudi women's team would sweep the medals.

For the first year I taught, I could not get over the idea that the students were dressed for a formal party rather than for class. (I was disabused of this notion when I saw them dressed for a party.) In a way, some of the classes did seem like parties, with the students displaying the same individuality and humor in their comments as they did in their dress. Class discussion never flagged, even when the topics were as abstruse as Dostoyevsky's idea of the conflict between the spirit and the flesh. In *The Idiot,* this conflict is symbolized by Prince Myshkin's inability to choose between two women, the soulful Aglaya and the voluptuous Nastasia. My students laughingly pointed out that a Muslim man would have no such problem: he could marry them both and let them fight it out between themselves.

But the students sparkled most in a class called Spoken English, a class I had originally dreaded teaching because it sounded so dull. I soon found out that in a class of twenty-five, I couldn't do much to correct individual pronunciation problems: I could only give them occasions for speaking English and for developing more confidence with the language. I gave them situations involving everyday conflicts to turn into skits, such as a conflict between a shopper and a preoccupied salesgirl. To my astonishment, they threw themselves into their parts, bringing props from home and even devising costumes not called for in the original outlines I had given them. They added male characters, for instance, wearing men's *taubs* or trousers and drawing on moustaches with eyebrow pencils. Even the girls who did not speak English very well joined in the spirit of the game. As a result, the frustrated lady shopper demanded to see the blouse in another color, and the salesgirl bunched her fingers at her in the Arab "wait-a-minute" gesture while cooing into the phone to her mustachioed admirer, "Oh, you must be very handsome. Drive around by my house tomorrow at seven so that I can look out of the upstairs window and see you."

The admirer, meanwhile, only needed to repeat, "Ah, my beauty, I love you" while the increasingly irritated shopper went through a list of colors in which she wanted to see the blouse.

When that got old, we went on to debates about such topics as whether families traveling abroad should take children with them. Discussion thrived, but the entire adversarial format of the debate quickly dissolved as the students took it over and made it fun.

One girl who was against traveling with children announced that children frequently annoyed the other passengers on an airplane. The last time she went on vacation, she pointed out, a child had kicked the back of her seat all the way from Jedda to London.

"When I got off the airplane," she noted, "I was walking like a crippled person. Everyone was saying, 'Who is the poor girl with the deformed back?' "

"Was it a little Pakistani boy about eight years old?" a girl on the opposing team wanted to know.

"How did you know?"

"Because normally he is seated behind me. He kicked my seat all the way from Riyadh to Athens last summer."

"I too know this child," a teammate of the first girl added. "I believe he takes a salary from the government. It is a way of discouraging girls from traveling even when they have permission."

"It's a way of keeping men from marrying us," another went on. "They see us leaving the airplane and think, 'I must not ask for the hand of the daughter of so and so, no matter what my mother recommends. She cannot walk, poor thing.' "

I had dreaded the essay-writing class almost as much as I had Spoken English, equally groundlessly. I figured it would be as dull as freshman composition in the States, only worse, because the students would make all of the second-language student grammar mistakes that I had never been taught how to explain. I would not be able to say anything to them except, "Trust me. This is not correct English." (My background was in American literature, not English as a second language, but the university had decided that all the spoken and written English classes for English majors should be taught by native speakers of the language, regardless of their training.)

As it turned out, I was right about the grammar mistakes but not about the dullness of the essays. They were delightful. Some of my delight came from the quaintness of the language, I must admit, but a great deal also came from the high spirits of the writers and the insights they gave me into their society. They had great fun, for instance, with classification and comparison and contrast themes, which enabled them to satirize people they disliked. Since they were working in rhetorical forms very different from those of their own culture, the organizational structures were sometimes a little overdone, but the humor and inventiveness came though anyway.

One girl categorized her classmates by their behavior in the lunch line and provided identifying characteristics of each type. The lunch line was always bedlam, because many of the students only had a few minutes between classes to grab a sandwich. Imagine a campus fast-food restaurant during the lunch crush if there were only one serving line and one cashier instead of half a dozen and if the patrons could select the wrapped sandwiches themselves instead of having a food worker hand the sandwiches to them. Worse, because many of the students could talk to their friends face-to-face only at school, the line was also clogged with students just chatting. They seldom went out in public and were not allowed to drive, remember, and those who had a driver normally had to share his services with the other women in their families.

Actually, when I braved the lunch mob myself, I did better than most, because I was tall enough to reach over the heads of most of the other would-be diners and grab the sandwich I wanted. I did feel sorry for the cashier, though, who had to cope with a dozen girls impatiently waving money in her face while she attempted to ring up each bill. It would have driven me berserk. As it was, the overall effect was a swirl of shiny black hair and green skirts, jingling jewelry, flashing red fingernails, a cacophony of voices shouting in three different languages, and the blended scents of garlic, chicken, and Obsession. I'd stagger back to my office just to recover from the sensory overload.

So naturally I was curious to see how my student would describe both the scene and the different types of patrons. In the first category, she said, were "the girls who used their strength to push to the front of the line as soon as it was known that food was available." These girls wore spike heels with closed toes, the better to trample the feet of their rivals while protecting their own appendages. Frequently, however, they ended up with whipped cream in their hair from lunging at the dessert trays. The sneaky types, on the other hand, ingratiated themselves with the foreign cafeteria workers and persuaded them to put food aside for them and even bring it to their tables, while category one was fighting its way through the line. These students were identifiable by their ability to say, "How pretty you look this morning" and "Please accept this small gift" in Korean, Tamil, Somali, and every other major Asian and African language. The third group patiently waited its turn. "These polite girls can be known by their thinness, because they never get any lunch."

The next time I went to the cafeteria, I looked around and observed more carefully. She was right.

I also liked another student's advice on the selection of a husband. One wants, she explained, to marry "the good temper man" and avoid "the bad temper man." Then she proceeded to distinguish between the behavior of the two by comparing the responses of her brother and her cousin when the family was on vacation in Spain and the tour bus that was supposed to take them to the beach never showed up. Her brother, the "good temper man" was "jokefull." (I never knew quite what to do about these neologisms that *ought* to be words. "Jocular" isn't quite the same.) He amused everyone except the cousin and his wife with improbable stories about what had happened to the bus driver.

"He saw some pretty Spanish lady walking in the street and is following her to her house to ask her father for her hand. The father is saying, 'No. you are just a bus driver.' Let us go there and endorse his character so that he can come take us to the seaside." And finally, when the driver still didn't show up, he observed his sisters' boredom and said, "You did not come from Riyadh to sit in a hotel lobby, did you? You are not happy. Let me call a taxi to take you shopping."

The "bad temper man," on the other hand, blamed his wife for the fact that they had come to Spain for a vacation in the first place, and "shouted her with impolite words until she was in miserable condition." At the time I was married to an American "bad temper man" who would have behaved in just the same way, and I was curious about how to identify and avoid this type before marriage. I was particularly interested in how a Saudi woman avoided this universal bane, because she would only have met a future husband on formal occasions, when he was on his best behavior. When the student came in talk about her paper, I asked her about these significant omissions. How do you know if you are getting a "good temper man?"

That's simple, she told me. Just ask his sister. If he is rude to his sister, he will be rude to his wife. Of course, as we discussed, a sister might misrepresent a very nice brother if she thought the questioner wasn't good enough for him, or she might praise a "bad temper man" if she thought the match would be in her family's interest. Yet on the whole, this struck me as excellent advice, which Western women would be wise to follow. Why hadn't I thought of that? But this brought up another point, as my husband had been an only child. What if he didn't have a sister?

"Then don't marry him. He has never learned about women."

When the school day was over and the students were again trans- formed into black veils getting into white cars, I thought once more of how anonymous they all became: all that humor, insight, and vitality was reduced to a bundle of black cloth. When I first went to Saudi Arabia, it was hard for me even to realize that there was a person inside the veiling, much less imagine that the person might be pleasant and interesting. When I got stuck in the women's compartment of a bus shortly after my arrival, I was startled when the black form beside me suddenly advised me, in correct if accented English, that the buzzer was jammed and I needed rap on the partition to tell the driver to stop.

In any society, what you see first is its exterior, its veil, and it is difficult for any newcomer to imagine that real people live beneath that veil. We see people in the street or overhear snatches of conversation or talk to taxi drivers and hotel desk clerks. English teachers like me visit the England of *Masterpiece Theater* and the France of Hemingway and Fitzgerald and imagine that we have actually seen a foreign country. Our society's veil, I suppose, is TV America, which can be as opaque to visitors as the black silk encasing Saudi women. In Saudi Arabia, the veils are simply more literal. And yet, when the literal veils come off, we are not necessarily prepared to see one another any more clearly.

Whenever Americans held forth about the cruelty of Arab men and the oppression of Arab women, I would think of my student and her "jokefull" brother sitting in a hotel lobby in Spain. If any of those Americans had seen the family, would they know they were seeing a young professional man kidding around with his sisters? The brother might be wearing a *taub*, he might be wearing trousers, but in either case he would be identifiable as an Arab because he would be speaking in Arabic. The girls beside him, my student and her sisters, might be wearing below-the-knee skirts rather than ankle-length ones, but they would probably have had their hair covered. The "bad temper" cousin and his wife would be off to one side, the unfortunate wife staring down at the carpet and blinking back the tears. Would the Americans walking by see two very different sorts of men and stop, at least, to wonder which was more typical, or would they just see a couple of rich Arabs with their harems?

5

❦

Borderline Women

During my first year of teaching in Saudi Arabia, I had three exceptional students, all North Africans, two of whom my American eye first classified as black and one whom I thought of as white. In Arab terms, however, they were *aswad shuwayah* (a little bit black), *asmar shuwayah* (sort of brown), and *shai-b-laban shuwayah* (sort of the color of tea with milk). These are not the only shades, of course. There is also *abiad shuwayah* (sort of white) and *qimhi shuwayah* (sort of wheat colored, which apparently means about the color of whole wheat flour.) The modifier *shuwayah* always makes the color more indefinite, so that even the shades of color and meaning blur. That one person was a little darker or lighter than another didn't really matter that much; everything was approximate. And so was the degree to which they were all Arabs, because in each case there was at least one other layer of culture that helped to define how they saw themselves and the world. All of these subtle blendings and complexities are lost the minute one uses terms like black and white, or Arab and Western.

Sakina

Sakina was taking a creative writing course from me because she wanted to find a form in which to write about her memories of growing up in Khartoum. Apparently, she came from a prominent Sudanese family, because she had been educated at a private academy where English was the language of instruction. In her file, I found letters of recommendation from teachers with hyphenated British names who praised her command of the language and her knowledge of British literature.

Sakina was a striking woman. Tall and slender, with delicate features and light brown skin *(shuwayah)*, she always wore a *taub*, the

31

traditional northern Sudanese dress, yards of brightly colored chiffon wound around her like a sari. And as far as I could tell, she always wore a different *taub:* one day she would be in yellow and brown, the next day in vivid green and blue, and another time in maroon with a subtle silver lamé stripe. Some of her cattier teachers referred to her as the Heracleitus of the Sudan, because she never stepped into the same *taub* twice. Instead of covering every lock of hair with a black scarf when she went outside, like the Egyptian and Saudi girls did (I called their outfit the Darth Vader look), she simply draped a fold of her *taub* over the top of her head, revealing most of her hairdo while the colors looked pretty next to her face. And out of the mouth of this vision of exotic loveliness came perfect upper-class British English.

Her writing was the same blending of cultures. In elegant and supple prose, she wrote her about widowed grandmother, who lived in a big house in Khartoum and held the whole family in fear. This formidable dowager had broken the engagement of another granddaughter, when she and her parents had the temerity to announce the engagement without first consulting her. In a rage, she refused to give her blessing, even though "the match was suitable in every other way." (This sounded a great deal like the language of Jane Austen to me.) Sakina's grandmother, thin, straightbacked, determined (I imagined her as Sakina grown old), refused to be mollified. Her rights had been infringed upon, her rights as the matriarch of the family. And so the engagement was broken. It was just too much bad luck to risk marrying without her consent.

Having heard all the usual things about the inferior status of women in Muslim countries, I was taken aback. As Sakina and I discussed this, I discovered that her grandmother's authority was by no means unusual, although her unforgiving resentment of slights to that authority was all her own. "I don't know why Westerners have the idea that Muslims see women as inferior," she told me. "Our Prophet teaches us, 'Your duty is to your mother—and to your mother and to your mother—and then to your father.' " In fact, she went on to say, one reason Muslim women usually preferred to have many children was that all their adult children would be on their sides if disputes arose within the extended family. "Preferred to have." I had always supposed that Muslim women had no choice in the matter. She explained it all to me quite patiently, apparently used to setting Westerners straight about Muslim society.

What startled me more, however, was her account of a *zar.* Because her grandmother lived near the academy where Sakina was going to school and her parents lived thirty or so miles away, Sakina stayed with her grandmother during the school year. She gradually became aware of unusual occurrences in the house. One day, the servants would spend the morning preparing food, and musicians would arrive at the house. Then for several days afterward, her grandmother would stay in her room, all her meals taken up to her on a tray. Then she would reappear again just as though nothing had happened, refusing to discuss any of what had taken place with Sakina. Sakina knew that this was called a *zar*, but she did not know what a *zar* was. She thought it was probably some sort of married women's party, and that the rich food and excitement must upset her grandmother's stomach. That her grandmother didn't want anyone to see her when she was sick just seemed like another of her eccentricities.

Nevertheless, Sakina was curious and resolved to sneak back to the house rather than go to school the next time her grandmother held a *zar*. She hid, she explained, in the pantry. I had a hard time imagining the house in my mind's eye, as words like "pantry" called up an image of an old British mansion and all the Arab homes I had seen in Saudi Arabia were just like you would see in any wealthy suburb in the States. What would an old house in Khartoum look like? But I could see Sakina among the brooms and dusty cans and jars of a pantry, her schoolbooks at her side, afraid to turn on the light to study for fear of being caught.

Then the drums began, a hypnotic beat at a slowly increasing tempo. At first, Sakina just listened through the door, but when she heard the movements of women dancing and the shrill *zaghrouta* (the high-pitched, ulalating cry that Arab women customarily make at celebrations), she decided that they were too involved to notice her. As she opened the door a crack, a wave of incense and music overwhelmed her. Her grandmother's friends, all dressed in their best clothes and jewelry, were dancing barefoot, everyone making up her own dance to the beat of the drum, her eyes glazed. "I realized that I could have walked into the room with them then and no one would have noticed me," she wrote. They were neither drinking wine nor smoking drugs, Sakina said, but later, when she saw people drunk, she thought they looked like these women. The music itself had made them drunk.

Then, to her shock, her grandmother appeared in the midst of the dancing women, dressed in her dead husband's military uniform and swinging his walking stick over her head in time to the music. "It was as though she were him," Sakina wrote. The gestures, the facial expressions, were all his, and yet the woman before her was still her grandmother, her gray hair pulled back in a bun below her military cap.

Sakina simply described the event, never mentioning what she herself understood from it. "Of course," she told me when we discussed her essay, "My grandmother believed that her husband's spirit entered her body and that she did become him." As for what she herself thought, she was reluctant to say. I was curious if her grandmother's harsh treatment of the family might have come from a sense that she was acting as her husband, but to this Sakina would only say, "Perhaps."

Later, I found that the *zar* was common throughout Sudan, southern Egypt, and Somalia. But no one could give me a clear understanding of what the practice was or where it originated. At first I thought it might be a Sufi ceremony, but northern Egyptians and Saudis assured me that the practice was not only un-Islamic, but *haram,* sinful. That made me wonder if it might have its roots in some of the animist religions of sub-Sahara Africa; certainly, what Sakina described sounded like some sort of religious ecstasy. Yet in this respect, it also sounded like some of the Dionysian cults of ancient Greece, especially as the participants were exclusively women. In fact, when I taught *The Bacchae* in my world literature course, an Egyptian student said, "Oh, I see. It is a *zar.*" The resemblance may have been coincidental. Yet whatever it was, it suggested to me that the distinctions between the cultures and peoples of Mediterranean Europe, Arab/Islamic North Africa, and sub-Sahara Africa are not as sharp as traditional historians would have us suppose. I sometimes wished my training had been in anthropology instead of literature, so that I could explore some of the relationships among the folk customs of these seemingly different cultures.

An ideal person to do this, obviously, would have been Sakina herself. Yet she didn't seem to think this was within her abilities or ambitions. When I asked her whom she imagined as her audience for her memoirs, she just said, "You, of course. I want to get a high mark in this class. And maybe keep it for my own memories." Had she thought about writing for a Western audience, to explain her culture? To that, she replied that I was interested because I knew her, but she didn't think any other Westerners would want to know what it was like to grow up in Sudan in the 1970s. Unfortunately, she may have been right. At any rate, I lost track of her after she graduated. Her husband, I knew, was a doctor at the university hospital, and after his contract expired they probably returned to Khartoum.

Hala

Hala's work was all the more remarkable because she seemed to me at first to have been so sheltered from what I had thought of as "the real world." In her native Egypt and in Saudi Arabia both, she went from her home to school and saw few people other than her classmates and family. Dressed in her ankle-length skirt and speaking her precise, slangless English, she seemed like a Victorian young lady, another character out of Jane Austen. And she was very small, only about five feet tall, with tiny, protruding bones and large brown eyes. Although she was twenty-two years old when I met her, she looked about sixteen.

Having just read a half-dozen stories that made all the usual beginning writers' mistakes, I was unprepared for her first story. Uncle Tarboush, whose real name no one knew anymore, showed up at the house every Friday afternoon to drink a cup of coffee with the family and to brag about the days when he had fought against the British. He had led rallies and shouted, "Down with colonialism!" He had worn his *tarboush* (fez) and *gellabeyah* when the British declared that the natives must wear Western clothes. I had seen enough Egyptian movies by now with my Egyptian neighbor, Zainab, to be able to picture him, I thought, even though my mental image didn't quite fit Hala's description. There was a fat, pug-nosed Egyptian comedian who always played the part of a buffoonish relative, so it was he that I saw heaving himself into the best chair and sipping his Turkish coffee with exaggerated delicacy. In the story, the children giggled at his funny clothes and especially at his *tarboush*, which they hid. There was a lot of funny business about the hat and repartee between him and the older kids that kept the story from getting maudlin—pretty well done, I thought. And even though the adults tolerated him only out of politeness, he was aware of what was going on and gently mocked them just as he had done with the kids. I liked this reversal of stereotype.

Then, as he was leaving one Friday, a car came speeding up the alley. Oh, no, I thought, she's going to kill him off and ruin this nice little story. Why does every beginning writer have to kill off her characters? I used to tell my students back in the States that they were not allowed to kill anyone for at least the first two stories, and I regretted not having made the same decree here.

But she didn't kill him off. The car just knocked him down and the driver and the passersby yelled at him for not watching where he was going. The *tarboush* was lying in the dusty street. I hadn't been to Cairo yet, so I had no idea just how dirty that street would have been, even though Hala had mentioned the chickens scattering in panic at the approach of the car. Slowly, he dusted himself off, put his *tarboush* back on, and walked away with as much dignity as he could muster.

I thought it was a well-crafted, realistic little story, although somewhat slight, until I went to Cairo a few months later and saw the statue of Sa'ad Zaghroul, the Egyptian nationalist leader exiled and imprisoned by the British. He looked just like her description of Uncle Tarboush. The story had a whole level of fantasy and political allegory that I had missed by not knowing Egyptian history, or indeed anything about the history of colonialism in the Arab world.

I also had not been taught much about the history of ancient Egypt, since the world history courses I had taken as an undergraduate all focused on Greece and Rome. This caused me at first to miss some of the complexity of her second story, in which she again combined realism and fantasy in her own variation of magic realism, although the term was not yet in vogue. This story was about Tiya, a girl living in Alexandria, who walked along the Mediterranean winter beaches imagining the sunboats of the ancient Egyptians, constructing a sunboat for herself in her mind's eye as she looked out at the gray Mediterranean. The scene then shifted to ancient Egypt, where workmen were constructing a sun boat to take Queen Tiya to the afterlife. But within the story, the sunboat was not death, but the power of the artist. The story ended with the modern day Tiya's imaginary sunboat taking literal form as she finished it in her mind and sailing away with her across a sea of reflected sunlight.

I later found out that Tiya was one of the Nubian queens of Egypt and the mother of Akhnaton, the pharaoh who tried to make the worship of the sun god the center of Egyptian religion. I also realized for the first time that Hala was probably a Nubian herself, as she was *aswad shuwayah*, unlike most other northern Egyptians. She was not from the tribal Nubians of Upper Egypt but from the Nubians who had come to work in the Mediterranean ports during colonial times. This seemed in keeping with the story's sense of exile and its theme of the imaginative reconstruction of a homeland and an identity.

Nor was this entirely artistic license. Later, when I was living in Egypt, I learned that traces of pharonic culture still abide in the folklore of Egypt, from the custom of children throwing their baby teeth to the sun, to the Abu Hejaj festival in Luxor where worshipers still carry sunboats through the city streets from one pharonic temple to another, to the Upper Egyptian peasant belief that when a good person dies, the gravedigger will see a tiny green boat come to take the person's spirit to paradise. This was part of why Hala could fit the image of the sunboat so naturally into her story.

Yet there was another layer of culture overlying the pharonic and the Egyptian, the Nubian and the Arab, that enabled her to express these ideas in English and in the form of a literary short story. She was also Western. None of these identities excluded the other; it was the multiple layers of culture that gave her writing such power and complexity. I have come to think that it is the person who only knows one culture and refuses to imagine any other who is truly sheltered from the real world.

Later, in fact, she told me things about the "real world" of Saudi Arabia that many Westerners who lived there never seemed to realize. After graduating, she worked for a couple of years as an interpreter at a dental clinic, translating between Saudi patients and English-speaking dentists. The patients were usually poor, often Bedouins, who had terrible dental problems because they never used toothbrushes, but instead cleaned their teeth with a kind of twig, called a *miswak*, that damaged the gums and scratched the enamel. Many of the British and American dentists had a very cavalier attitude toward their patients, figuring that they'd pulled a fast one on the Arabs by getting close to twice the salary they would be getting at home while doing as little work as possible.

One old man came in with a terrible abscess about an hour before the clinic closed. Instead of trying to do something for him then, the dentist just scheduled a cleaning, telling the old man that his mouth was too dirty for them to work on. "Normally," Hala told me, looking down at her hands, "I do not translate abuse, but this time I did. I told the dentist, 'Your patient tells you that to leave him in such pain, you are the son of a thousand dogs and your mother is a diseased prostitute.' " I can imagine how difficult it was for her to repeat this, however euphemistic her translation may have been. The dentist just laughed.

What disturbed her more was the situation of the Filipina dental assistants, many of whom were actually dentists but found that they could earn more as dental assistants in the Gulf. These women were locked in their dormitories whenever they were not at work. It was as if they were in jail, Hala told me. But they told her they were much better off than the domestic workers, who were sometimes refused medical care when they got sick, insulted and even beaten by their employers, and often unpaid. The Filipinas she knew accepted this with a kind of resigned stoicism, as if this were simply the way of the world. This haunted her, she told me. But as far as I know, she never wrote about it.

Nada

Born in Michigan of Egyptian parents, Nada had lived there until she was fifteen, when her parents decided to go back to Egypt. But even in the far more restrictive Saudi Arabia, where her father went next, she was an American. She had to wear the regulation long green skirt to the women's college, of course, but she always topped it with a T-shirt, usually with a funny slogan on it. Eschewing the spike-heeled sandals of the Saudi students, she wore white ankle socks and sneakers. She also avoided make-up and jewelry and wore her hair stuck back in a pony tail most of the time. This made it all the more remarkable that she managed to look not bad even among the dazzlingly coifed and bejeweled Saudi girls, who wanted to look their most spectacular in case one of their classmates had an eligible brother. But what I noticed first about her was her voice, not only the mid-Western accent and the slang, but the volume, just a tiny bit louder than was considered suitable for a well-brought up young lady. Nada was determined to make herself heard.

"Talk about culture shock," she told me about her first return to Egypt. "The part about picking up the language was kind of fun. My Mom would send me out to do the shopping, buying vegetables and stuff from the open-air markets. The vendors all thought it was really funny that I looked like an Egyptian but spoke Arabic like a *khawaga*, a foreigner. But it was all pretty good natured. What really freaked me out was the stuff about guys. My parents had told me all this stuff about how it was such a big sin and scandal not to be a virgin when you got married here, so I just thought, 'Ok, no problem. I don't particularly want to do that anyway.' But I used to like to hang around the courtyard at the American University in Cairo and talk to guys. Big no-no. You're not supposed to talk to guys unless you've been introduced. Going out for a cup of coffee is a date, and that means you're really serious. And you can't go out on a real date unless you're engaged to the guy. I kept thinking, 'This isn't real.' I used to sleep with my American passport under my pillow. When my parents grounded me for talking to guys, I remember yelling at them, 'You can't do this to me. I'm an American citizen.' "

She laughed when she told me these things. At first, she would just stop by my office to talk, but later she would come to my apartment, wearing jeans or a short skirt underneath her *abaya*, to show me what she had been writing. Because she wrote feature articles for one of Riyadh's English-language newspapers, one of our favorite pasttimes was comparing what she had written, with all her subtle jibes about the treatment of women and foreign workers, with the blandly sanitized versions that appeared in print. Sometimes an allusion would escape the editor, such as her remark that the "guest workers" were as happy and well-treated as the "darkies" in the Old South. Finally, however, the paper either got tired of editing out her criticisms, or the editors began to realize that she was implying criticism they could not always catch, because they abruptly stopped using her work.

However, freed from the constraints of writing for a highly censored press, her writing became far more complex and provocative. Late that spring, both of us were disturbed by the Saudi media's presentation of the so-called "Filipino crime." Two Filipino house servants were accused of murdering their Lebanese employer and raping his wife. The press noted, almost in passing, that the two men had not been paid for months, that they had been denied permission to return to the Philippines despite the fact that their contracts had expired, and that they had been "abused." (According to rumor, they had been homosexually raped by the employer and his friends.)

What the media focused upon was the confession—a reenactment of the crime by the men themselves, using dummies as victims. This aired a half-dozen times a day on Saudi television, even after the two Filipinos had been executed. It was impossible to miss it. Yet the English version of the confession, made by the men themselves, did not coincide with the Arabic translation. Concerning the alleged rape of the woman, the Filipino man repeated, "But I did not continue," but the Arabic version reported him confessing to the rape. What bothered Nada and me more was how that confession tape came to be made. Had they been promised clemency if they made it? Had they been tortured? Were they guilty at all? Often, men were executed in the square in front of the Dira mosque, but their crimes were not announced until the time of their execution. Never before had confessions been shown on television, which made me wonder if the tape was shown so frequently to counter rumors of their innocence. Or could it have been done to fan racial prejudice against Filipinos, who were better organized than many of the other foreign workers? Whatever the causes, it was a brutal travesty of justice transformed by the media into something excusable. And neither of us could do anything about it.

Nada wrote eloquently about all of this and more: the slavery of foreign servants that was virtually taken for granted, the absence of any labor laws in Saudi Arabia to protect foreign workers from exploitation and abuse, the absence of public trials, the absence of any international human rights groups to protest what was going on, the silence of the Western press. Unlike me, Nada could imagine the lives of the two men, because the same things happened to poor Egyptians when they came to the country: the grinding poverty, the ill-afforded bribes paid to middlemen to secure visas to Saudi Arabia, the joy of a whole family at having someone working in the Gulf, the hope this work meant. Now children would have school clothes, old people would have medical care, and young women would be spared lives of prostitution. Then the actual arrival: locked inside the house, denied the work permits needed to leave the house even if they could get out, denied pay, beaten, homosexually raped. Not only were they slaves, but none of the money that made them come to Saudi Arabia in the first place ever got back to the family. Then the employer was murdered. Either they did it, or they were simply convenient scapegoats. They were tortured until they confessed and then beheaded in the public square. Nada wondered how a person could continue living in comfort and security, when such things could happen to people not so different from oneself, just poorer and more desperate. Worst of all, no one cared, because the accused men were poor and foreign—throwaway people. My hands shook as I read her essay. I didn't have any answers either.

After she graduated, Nada was able to make a deal with her parents. She could go back to the United States and work on a master's degree in journalism. But in return, they wanted her to live with her uncle and his family, who would expect her to follow more or less the same restrictions that a young single woman would in Egypt, namely, a nine o'clock curfew and a promise not to date. They also wanted her to be formally engaged to the suitable young man they had found for her back in Egypt, which I considered more of a sacrifice, although she didn't. "It's just a way for us to date and get to know each other," she pointed out. "Then if it doesn't work out, or one of us finds somebody else, we can break the engagement with no hard feelings." I thought it would be something of a challenge for her to "find someone else" if she couldn't date and wasn't allowed out after dark, but I didn't mention this.

Two years later, when I was back in Pennsylvania, I had a phone call from her late one night. Apparently, she had found someone else, an American who wanted to marry her and who did not seem to understand what it would do to her family if she married outside her religion. "I explained to him first of all that I couldn't go to bed with him because I had to be a virgin when I got married because of my religion. He said, 'Fine. Let's get married. You can have your religion, I can have mine, so what's the problem?' I tried to explain to him that a Muslim girl can't marry outside her religion and that my parents would be just devastated. It would be like I was spitting on them and every value they had. But Tom just said, 'Ah, they'll come around. You love me and I love you. It's worth the risk.' And that was when I realized that to an American girl, it would be worth the risk, but not to me."

"I thought you were an American girl," I said. This, after all, was the girl who had slept with her American passport under her pillow.

"So did I," she replied, "Until I came back here." Then she told me a story that to this day makes me furious every time I think about it. After one of her first journalism classes, the professor had drawn her aside and told her that he did not want Arabs in his class and that she had better drop it, because he wasn't about to pass her. It was so blatant that Nada thought the professor must be kidding. She attended all the classes and did all the work. Then she got her grade—a C, a failing grade in a graduate course. She asked her advisor if she could lodge a complaint against the professor for this, but he counseled her against it. The professor was very well placed in the department, he explained, and given Nada's undergraduate degree from an Arab university and her Arab surname, no one would believe her. Besides, he went on, the other Arab students were always whining about their grades, and she didn't want to associate herself with them, did she?

She told me that she thought of pointing out that she was an American, not an Arab, but that she suddenly realized it wasn't true.

It didn't matter that she was born in America, spoke American English, and had made American values a part of who she was. To Americans she was an Arab. And to them she could not be both Arab and American, or even Arab *shuwayah*. What disturbed her almost as much was that when she later told her American boyfriend about it, he just pointed out that after they were married, she would have his last name and nobody would need to know she was an Arab.

I could understand why she decided to go back to Egypt and marry her Egyptian fiancé.

I had news of Hala and Nada over the years, but not of Sakina. Both of them abandoned whatever goals they might have had for writing careers. I can't help thinking that this was the West's and indeed the world's loss, at least in a small way, if not precisely the West's or the world's fault. Many promising young writers never develop the literary and marketing skills, the self-confidence, or the persistence they need to publish their work. Many young women all over the world have been taught to put their families above their professional aspirations, which may not be entirely wrong. It wasn't even precisely what happened in Nada's case. And many people are discriminated against and find it only makes them angrier and more determined. Yet Sakina, Hala, and Nada were unique voices all, writers who had mastered at least two cultures in ways in which few others can even understand one. They could write from inside North African and Middle Eastern cultures as almost no Westerner could, and yet they could write in English, with an awareness of Western values. In their writing, they transcended boundaries and demolished stereotypes. Perhaps this asset was also one of their problems. To some extent, I wonder if they would have received more encouragement if they had known one culture only, if Nada had not been a brash, spunky American girl with an Arab face and name, if all of them had not in their very being called into question the distinction between us and them.

Hala's options were also limited by another fact: she suffered from a slight curvature of the spine—hardly noticable most of the time—but enough of an abnormalty to make her virtually unmarriagable by Egyptian standards. Whatever beauty of mind and spirit they all shared, they were defined by their bodies—perfect or not, Arab-looking or not, dark-skinned or light-skinned, female. And it was both Western and Arab society that judged them thus and found them wanting by some standard. I began to imagine that I understood the impulse behind the *zar*, which made women want to confine the spirits of powerful men within their own limited and defined bodies. All of them had tried to find some escape from the physical world that confined and defined them, and all escaped to imaginary worlds accessible only by sunboat—to the world of ancient Egypt, or to an equally imaginary America where everyone's rights were equal.

Nada's younger sister was a student of mine when I returned to Saudi Arabia in 1987. Nada was married, and she owned and operated a boutique in a fashionable section of Cairo. No, she no longer hoped for a career in journalism. Her husband was "a nice guy," but had trouble getting used to her American ways and attitudes. Things were working out all right, and, as she pointed out, most people don't get the lives they dream about when they're seniors in college.

Hala also came to the States and got a master's degree in literature. Apparently, she didn't run into the kind of discrimination Nada faced, either because of her less assertive personality or simply good luck. I saw her briefly when I was in Washington, but all she mentioned to me was that one of her Americans friends had told her that before meeting her, he had thought all Arabs were terrorists. The image of itty-bitty Hala hijacking a plane was certainly striking, but I was glad she had caused him to revise his opinion.

While I was teaching in China and later in Egypt, she wrote to me, usually about her classes and what she was reading, with occasional references to a heart problem, which she never characterized as serious. She went back to Egypt and found work as a translator in a business office of some kind, because she wasn't really interested in teaching. Then the letters stopped. I never knew why until I returned to Saudi Arabia and was talking to a former student, now a graduate assistant, who had known most of my other students.

Hala was dead. The previous winter, she had developed pneumonia, which was complicated by her heart problem. The hospital in Alexandria couldn't save her. But when I thought of her, I saw a sunboat rising into the air above the gray Mediterranean, taking her away across an ocean of light.

6

Home

I left Saudi Arabia with very mixed feelings. I liked my students and my colleagues, but I was disturbed by the arbitrariness of the Saudi government and the absence of basic human rights protection. Professionally, teaching in Saudi Arabia was good for me, but personal reasons (a last-ditch effort to save a failing marriage) impelled me to leave. I spent the following year teaching in the People's Republic of China and then went back to the United States. I wasn't happy teaching in the States again, however. I discovered that it was not precisely Saudi Arabia or China that I missed. It was the pieces of myself I had left in those places, and it was the knowledge and experience for which I now had no place for—parts of myself that would have to be thrown away if I were ever going to feel comfortable again in my own country.

On one level, I had been warned. The wife of an American foreign service officer had told me, "Nobody is going to want to know what happened to you. You'll say 'When I was in Ruritania during the coup attempt . . .' and people will interrupt you and say, 'Oh, while you were gone, they put in a shopping mall over on the east side.' Or they'll just yawn." Later, I read an Edith Wharton novella, *False Dawn*, that explained the feeling more precisely. A young man returning to America after years in Europe came to think of his whole European experience as a tightly packed suitcase. He couldn't take one thing out without everything else falling out too. But one item or two was all anyone wanted to see. Finally, he came to the bitter conclusion that the only thing to be done was to put the whole suitcase away in a dusty attic.

I didn't want to do this. Yet in a way, I could understand why I had a less than appreciative audience. My friends had no way of understanding either my experience or my need to talk about it. To them, I'm sure my talk about China and the Middle East seemed to be showing off. But what made me so glum was more than the fact that my travels and ruminations were not topics of mutual interest with my old friends or my new acquaintances. It was a hundred small things. The moment you have responded sympathetically to another culture is the moment you cease to accept your own society's structures as natural and unquestionable. I had come to enjoy not only speculating about why other cultures ordered things differently, but why American society is as it is. In China, walking with a Chinese friend past the old women selling popsicles from coolers, I had been startled by her remark that in America, she imagined, the popsicle ladies must have electric freezers. I could only begin to explain why we would have a vending machine instead, and what was lost and gained by this difference. If I was at first puzzled by the restrictions on young women in Muslim societies, I later came to think that it was also curious that in America we encouraged teenagers to date, celebrated sexuality in our media, and then were appalled when teenage girls became pregnant.

I missed those kinds of insights. I missed the friendly presence of people who had entirely different assumptions about the way the world worked but were curious to hear about mine. I missed always having a new puzzle to think about. America suddenly felt vast and blank and unconnected. At first, I thought that America had changed. And perhaps it had, a little bit. I left America at the tail end of the seventies and came back to a Reaganized America in which the single, desperate focus of college students seemed to be getting jobs when they graduated and somehow managing to pay back their student loans. Colleagues seemed equally single-minded in their pursuit of promotion and tenure. No one, as far as I could tell, was really much concerned about expanding his knowledge of the world around him. And no one seemed to have time for friendship. I say "seemed" because of course my vision was distorted. I had just spent three years arguing for a remembered and idealized America with Arabs and Chinese who had been taught that America was corrupt and materialistic. The fact that I could not find that remembered America reflected more the changes in me than in the country.

One thing that had changed about me were some of my opinions about teaching. Before, I had half-bought the student argument that if they had not learned to write a coherent paragraph after four years in public high schools, they could not be expected to master this skill in one semester of freshman comp. Now, having seen that people who spoke only Arabic or Chinese until they were fourteen were able to write perfectly acceptable English prose by the time they were twenty-two or twenty-three (my Arab and Chinese graduate students), it seemed to me that this feat should not be beyond the capacities of any native speaker of English who was intelligent enough to pass the college entrance exams. It struck me as a matter of motivation. This made me more impatient with student excuses and consequently somewhat less popular. And all the coping skills I had developed while teaching abroad no longer applied. It no longer worked to find mishaps quaint and amusing or the perpetrators of academic annoyances comic representations of their cultures, because these people were representatives of my own culture now. Nobody found it an amusing inspiration for banter, for instance, when the English department, running short of paper, issued weekly memos on this same scarce paper reminding department members of the paper shortage. How functional the "us and them" mentality of so many expatriates is.

I remember coming back from the library across a grove of oaks to my class one evening, feeling the light autumn rain, smelling the wet leaves underfoot, and thinking of all the years when I had walked across just such campuses. I would soon be teaching *My Antonia,* a world that seemed like the real America. The campus was still the real America in its smell and feel and sight. But something had gone out of it, and I could only feel nostalgia and a sense of absence. The sensory America and the fictional America seemed equally real and equally remote from the world in which the people around me lived. I was no longer of it.

I recalled another walk a year earlier, in Saudi Arabia. I was coming out of the English department building into the blazing March sunshine, trying to keep my high-heeled sandals from catching in the hem of my ankle-length skirt. Why was it, I wondered, looking at the groups of young women chatting and laughing on the steps of the library, that the students seemed happy and secure there in a way that most American students did not? I had just been talking to Nada about her childhood in America; suddenly I realized that the lack of freedom and the sense of security were linked. In Saudi society you either conformed to social norms or you made yourself a total outcast. In America, you had a confusing choice of lifestyles. And you could not trust anyone but yourself to decide which way was right—parents, tradition, all of them could be wrong. I thought of all the rebellious and confused young women who had confided in me over the years in the States, girls who were afraid they would never find jobs when they graduated, who were afraid they were pregnant, who had domineering boyfriends they were afraid to break up with because they thought no one else would ever be interested in them. Young adulthood certainly didn't seem to be a very happy time for most American women.

But did everything have to be planned? There on the sunny steps, I stopped and looked out over the scattered buildings and the clumps of palm trees and the paved walkways of the campus, and it seemed to me a metaphor for my students' lives. You followed the paved walkways; you went where everyone had gone and where everyone else was going. Then you were safe. But if I had followed America's paved walkways, I would not have been there in Saudi Arabia, much less have led the life and formed the ideas that had made me who I was. American society let me take shortcuts and wrong turns and still be a part of it, if I wanted to be. I could be in the midst of everything so different from my remembered America precisely because I was an American. If I no longer belonged as completely in America as I once had, I could still never be of anywhere else, or really want to be.

It was in this spirit that I decided to try to go back to the Middle East again, this time to Egypt.

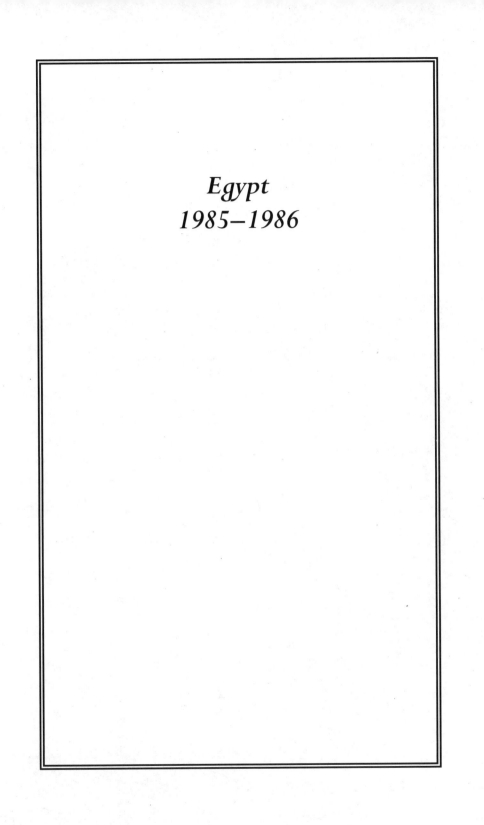

Egypt
1985–1986

7

⚭

Cairo

I arrived in Egypt in the full daylight of an early October afternoon, as good a metaphor as any for the difference between Egypt and Saudi Arabia. Noise and color and crowds and light and poverty—everything to make it the opposite of Saudi Arabia. The driver from the Fulbright Commission picked me up at the airport, and, unlike my first driver in Riyadh, he knew some English and wanted to chat. I wanted to look out the window at the people, people everywhere. Women in brightly colored dresses and headscarves, women in Western clothes, women with covered and uncovered hair walking arm-in-arm down the street, men in *gellabeyahs*, men in jeans, men in leisure suits, men and women carrying heavy loads on their backs or heads, men and women driving cars and donkey carts, people laughing and talking and yelling—and all out in public, in the street.

In Saudi Arabia, I had always felt very much on the periphery. I knew I was in the middle of a society perhaps more complex than I could understand, and one, I felt, that kept me at a distance from it. The Saudi university officials I met were polite, many of the Saudi students were friendly, and a few were willing to talk about their country, but there was always a certain reserve. Most of my friends were Egyptians and Palestinians, along with a few Brits and Americans; all were people who were also out of their element. Egypt felt like an accessible society.

Our first stop was the Fulbright office in Garden City, a once-classy section of the city with tree-lined streets and a view of the Nile. There, the brusque American woman director wanted to know if I had any questions, a rather odd inquiry, I thought, of a person who had just gotten off a fourteen-hour flight and wanted desperately to take a hot shower. But at the time, I was too tired to ask questions. No, other than where I was going to sleep that night, I didn't have any questions. Then why was I there bothering her, she wanted to know.

In a state of mild annoyance, I was driven off to the Fulbright apartment in Zamalek, another once-classy section of town that now seemed a bit dusty and run-down. As I had a map of Zamalek in my tour book and as it was only half past four by the time I had gotten washed up and unpacked, I decided to explore. It was already beginning to cool off, and a light wind rustled through the dusty trees. I walked down the main shopping street to the bridge across the Nile, over broken pavement and vendors selling fruit and vegetables on the sidewalks and stacks of evening newspapers being flung out into the streets in great bundles, all of which precluded contemplative strolling. One Egyptian newspaper columnist had suggested that the writer of the song "Walk like an Egyptian" must have visited Cairo, seen pedestrians trying to make their way along the broken pavement while simultaneously dodging the displays of street vendors, and concluded they were doing some kind of a dance.

Zamalek was everything mixed together at once, as was much of the rest of Cairo. Black-and-white taxis crawled up the street, waved at by a half-dozen different people, all hopefully shouting out their destinations. To this, the drivers would respond with a "tsk" and an upward jerk of the head if they weren't going in that direction. Donkey carts collecting rubbish made their way among the shiny white Mercedes in front of art deco apartment buildings. Along the street by the river and tucked away in side streets were Western-style bars and restaurants with dim lighting, potted plants, and English-speaking waiters. A block away, a man would be frying *taamia* (Egyptian felafel) on a rickety card table in the middle of the sidewalk in front of a cement-block eatery open to the street, while patrons sat at equally dilapidated card tables inside.

The Supermarket, for thus it proclaimed itself, was three aisles of somewhat dusty canned goods and imported cookies, a bin of pirated cassette tapes, and a home freezer full of popsicles. (I thought about writing to my Chinese friend that there were no popsicle ladies in Egypt. The only Middle Eastern equivalents that I could find were the canned soda ladies of the souks in Saudi Arabia.) Obviously, most people bought their food elsewhere, at the butcher shops that displayed lamb and beef carcasses out in front on big hooks and from the vegetable vendors, where everything was fresh and everything was bargained for. The clothing stores were all small enough to be run by the owners and reminded me of the stores in the small town in Pennsylvania where I had grown up thirty years before.

The streets were full of packs of laughing young men and women, the former examining the latter and the latter pretending to be more interested in the clothing displayed in the windows of tiny shops. This was westernized Cairo, and yet to the extent that it seemed like the West at all, it was the West of the 1950s rather than the 1980s, just like the stores themselves. The young women wore carefully color-coordinated outfits—matching shoes, purses, and earrings. The women were all in skirts; pants were only for the daring, because, as Egyptians later pointed out to me, pants revealed the contours of the body. The straight skirts and spike heels, however, also seemed to do a fairly good job of showing off the behinds of the wearers, so I took the ban on pants to be more a matter of convention than of modesty. Although every once in a while I saw a *hijab* (veil), it was usually only a brightly colored scarf covering some of the woman's hair but pulled back to show her earrings and a few locks of hair in the front. If its purpose were to make the woman more inconspicuous and less attractive to men, the heavy eye makeup seemed to work in the opposite direction. Some of the women turned to eye me critically and a little curiously. Clearly, I was underdressed for an evening stroll.

However much I just wanted to observe and consider everything that was going on around me, I quickly discovered that I myself was hardly invisible. Having lived in three different cultures in as many years, I found it odd how my appearance changed so radically from one to another. I felt like Alice in Wonderland. In China, I was so funny-looking that people would fall off their bicycles staring at me and little children would point and giggle. In the States, I was a reasonably attractive woman again, if rather ordinary-looking. Here in Egypt, I was suddenly transformed into an exotic beauty, if the repeated comments of *"ya helwa"* ("hey, beautiful") and *"ya asaal"* ("hey, honey") were any indication.

This was not as gratifying as one might suppose, because it was combined with unfortunate stereotypes about the availablity of American women, gleaned from American movies and TV shows. In fact, young urban Egyptian men seemed to react to me rather as the American men in the beer commercial respond when apprised of the arrival of the Swedish bikini team. The fact that I was ten or fifteen years older than most of them didn't seem a deterrence. I hadn't been the focus of so much attention from twenty-year-old men since my freshman year in college.

I quickly learned that ignoring them didn't work; they just thought I was hard of hearing and talked louder. My walks became more enjoyable after I learned to say "Behave yourself" and "Go away" in Arabic, commands with which they seemed reasonably willing to comply. Nevertheless, I have often felt that the greedy television executive who decided to syndicate *Dallas* in the Middle East should be transformed into a young light-haired American woman and forced to ride buses around Cairo until the last rerun disappeared from circulation.

Egypt is a contact culture. People speak to strangers, and one has to speak back, even if it's only "Behave yourself," to young mashers (the old-fashioned term seems appropriate here) or "Not today, thanks," to souvenir sellers, shoe shiners, and men selling boat rides. On the other hand, I repeatedly saw passersby intervene in quarrels, holding back men who flailed their fists and shouted curses at men similarly restrained, until finally each was led off in a different direction by someone telling him that he was in the right, but what could one do? The world was unfair.

Egyptians liked this. And I could see its charm. When Zainab's daughter, Reem, now a chubby nineteen year old, went out in a color-coordinated outfit of black and white (black skirt, black and white blouse, black earrings, black and white bag and shoes) she was immediately hailed by wags who pretended to mistake her for one of the city's black-and-white taxis. I cringed as I imagined the scene, the well-dressed girl making her way down the street, followed by a group of boys yelling, "Taxi! Taxi!" But instead of being embarrassed, she thought it was funny. As for me, I felt as if the world was out to meet me the moment I stepped out on the street, and I wasn't always in a mood to be met.

That afternoon, though, I was too dazed to be annoyed. I walked down to the bridge and looked out at the Nile, sparkling in the late afternoon sunlight. The Corniche was fairly deserted, young Cairo being more occupied with window shopping, and at last I had a moment to just look around me and convince myself that I was really there. To my left was a huge tourist hotel. I could still hear the traffic from the bridge and smell the exhaust fumes. But there were trees overhead—big, natural-looking trees, not pathetic seedlings set into little squares in the cement of the sidewalks, as in Riyadh. And here, it seemed to me, was a real society, with the rubbish on the street and sunlight on the Nile, evolving naturally out of itself for thousands of years, influenced by other cultures without becoming an artificial imitation of them.

8

Official Egyptians

Two weeks after I arrived in Egypt, I was on my way to Mansoura, a city in the eastern Nile delta, where I would be teaching. I was to make this trip many times, sometimes by bus, sometimes by intercity taxi. The latter was a Peugeot stuffed with as many passengers as the driver could garner and driven at breakneck speed, all at a cost of a couple of Egyptian pounds and, possibly, one's life. The bus, I thought, was safer, until it broke down a couple of times and left me to try to hitch a ride with one of the same "flying coffins" (so named for their speed and safety) that I had scorned before.

Now, I was with Asha, a plump and patronizing Egyptian woman from the Fulbright commission who advised me to wash vegetables and fruits carefully before eating them and to avoid overtipping the *bauwab* (janitor), who was supposed to run errands for the tenants, keep strangers out of the building, and take away the garbage. Later, when the *bauwab* carried a refrigerator up seven flights of stairs on his back, she told me that a tip of twenty-five piasters (less than a quarter) would be adequate. Apparently, Asha thought it her business to see that the lower classes didn't get spoiled by unthinking Americans. But I can't be too ironic about her because, like a fool, I actually followed her instructions.

Now, I was looking out the window at the incredibly green countryside flashing past. I was never very far outside of Riyadh when I was in Saudi Arabia, having only made few excursions into the desert, so looking at rural Egypt, it was China rather than Saudi Arabia I compared it to: the same crowds of people everywhere, even out in the country, and the same backbreaking farm work being done by hand. But the Egyptian farmers looked healthy and I didn't see the bent old women I had seen in China, probably because in Egypt farm women carried loads balanced on their heads rather than on their backs. In China, everyone I saw, except for a few party officials, was bone thin, and during the winter even my students looked malnourished. Even though many of my Egyptian students were the sons and daughters of farmers and working-class city people, they were adequately fed and clothed. And here, donkeys or buffalo turned the irrigation wheels, not gangs of people. Donkeys and buffalo also occasionally shared the roadway with cars, although usually only by crossing it, loaded with heaps of clover, which made them look like those pottery animals that grow coats of curled cress when you water them.

There were fields, and people working in those fields, harvesting clover with sickles. Each family's plot of land was too small, I guessed, to justify the expense of farm machinery, even if they had the money. Some of the houses also must have lacked running water, because women were washing clothes in the canal that ran alongside the highway. I suggested this to Asha.

"They do, but they wash in the canal out of habit. These people are very backward," she said with a sigh.

Later, I found that I was right, and that her Marie Antoinette attitude was all too common among middle-class Cairenes. These same canals, in which people were washing their clothes, their farm animals, and themselves, were filled with bilharzia snails, carriers of a deadly parasitic disease that kills thousands of Egyptian villagers every year. Instead of testing and treating the villagers or installing a functioning water system, the Egyptian government had launched a television ad campaign advising farmers to stay away from the canals, even though the only televisions the villagers might see were in cafés. Not surprisingly, perhaps, the ad contained no recommendations for how else people were supposed to get water. As in China, the real money went to the military; Egypt just had less to show for it.

And yet, and yet. People did not look miserable. Children with dirty bare feet but clean faces waved at the cars. In the market towns, people laughed as they bargained for vegetables. Again and again, I would see what looked at first like a fight breaking out and then see from the men's laughing faces that it was just horseplay. None of this, however, relieved Asha's gloom or boredom.

"How much does a donkey cost?" I asked suddenly, as a child on a donkey moved to the side of the road to let us pass. Surely even these poor farmers must have had a little extra money or else they would be walking.

"What?" she gasped. "How can you ask such a thing? I am not a peasant."

"Just curious," I said.

"Are you thinking about buying one?" She asked acidly.

Official people almost always show a country at its worst; as far as I can tell, bureaucrats and officials from all countries take a special rudeness and stupidity exam, with those scoring highest in these traits assigned to work for the China Internal Travel Service or at Customs and Passport Control at Kennedy Airport; but the Fulbright Commission in Egypt was not far down on the list. After Asha and the director, I thought, everyone I met would seem pleasant.

But the next Egyptian I met was the jovially pompous department chairman. Zainab, who knew him, had written to me that he embodied Egyptian academia at its worst, although it was several months before I realized this for myself. In the entire school year, I never once saw him reading a book or explaining an idea to a student. Instead, he seemed to spend most of his office time talking on the phone. Like many Egyptian academics, he held posts at several different universities in order to make a living wage and spent a great deal of time traveling between them, appearing for one lecture, missing another. Some of his graduate student assistants nicknamed him "the satellite" because, they said, he was in constant orbit—one caught a glimpse of him and then he was gone. Indeed, he never descended from the stratosphere long enough to read their masters theses or help them teach the courses in which they were supposed to be assisting him but which in fact they were teaching entirely on their own.

Nevertheless, at that first meeting he was cordial, and so was the pretty young teacher, Noura, who lived in the building next to mine and was there to greet me when I arrived. I liked her. For one thing, her cordiality was rather remarkable, considering that she had been more or less roped into being my official friend by the chairman. She was also about to start teaching for the first time and had just become engaged, so being a companion to a strange foreign woman was probably not high on her wish list. But because she was both good-natured and well-brought-up, she very kindly came over to check on me, helped to show me around the city, and introduced me to some of her English-speaking friends. Suddenly, I felt I was actually talking to a version of the color-coordinated young ladies I had seen window shopping in Zamalek. She was a step beyond official people and knowing her put me a step beyond viewing Egypt from the window of a car.

She was helpful. Unlike the chairman, she joked with me instead of condescending to me, even though I seemed to have startled her with all my questions about Egypt. (Apparently, the proper professorial attitude was to feign complete knowledge of all things and insist on one's views even when dead wrong.) Because she was fun, I later sought her advice when I tried to disguise myself as an Egyptian in hopes of cutting down on the number of mashers when I went to Cairo. This was at least remotely possible, I thought, because some Egyptian women did have brown hair and blue eyes, albeit they were a small minority. So instead of wearing my usual slacks and blazer, I dressed up like the young women I had seen in Cairo—skirt, earrings, dressy blouse, pantyhose. I thought it was a remarkable impersonation. But Noura threw up her hands when she saw me. "No, Doctor. You do not look like an Egyptian. You look like an American." Then she pointed out to me the inadequacy of my ensemble: my running shoes ("Only an American would wear such shoes") and my beaten-up brown leather purse. Pumps and a matching bag were my ticket. I tried it and discovered that I got compliments in Arabic rather than propositions in English—a step in the right direction, at least. To be as inconspicuous as I wanted to be, I feared I would have to start wearing a headscarf and a long skirt, which would have made me seem so silly to myself that I would have felt like a spectacle even if I weren't one.

Despite Noura, I was still seeing Egypt from the outside during those first weeks in Mansoura, and I was lonely. I had a huge apartment in a modern-looking building, which, after everyone left that first afternoon, I discovered I shared with several hundred cockroaches. "Spray Raid," Noura advised, and talked the *bauwab*'s wife into sweeping up the corpses for me after I had done so. This cut the population in half, but I would still find a half-dozen of them in the middle of the kitchen floor, lying on their backs and kicking, whenever I came back from school. So I tried to concentrate instead on the view from my balcony, where mists rose from the Nile every morning and the sun set every night. From my balcony, I would also watch the fishermen's boats go out in the morning and the children playing soccer in the park in the evening until I began find pleasure in the isolation akin to that sheer beauty.

9

Class Wars

All of the Egyptians I met at first were upper or upper-middle class. Of course gradually, as I got to know more people, especially those students and teachers who sought my friendship rather than those who were stuck with me, I calmed down enough to realize the limits of my generalizations about "the Egyptian character." For one thing, the only Egyptians with whom I could carry on a real conversation were people who spoke English. Most of them were either college students or college professors, hardly a representative group in any society. And the sorts of people who make a point of befriending foreigners are usually not typical either; if my observations are correct, they are either unusually curious and open-minded students of human nature or they are such socially inadequate bumblers in their own culture that they need a foreigner around to make them feel functional. At least those were the types that I seemed to attract.

The campus itself, where I was to meet most of my students and colleagues, was a run-down collection of cement block buildings crowded with benches instead of desks and lecture halls designed for fifty students filled with a hundred. Some students brought their own folding chairs from home. As in China, I had to speak from a podium on a raised platform, which made me feel as though I were on stage, and students propped cassette recorders against the podium so they could replay the lecture.

But there the resemblance ended. My Chinese students often wrote English well but had problems speaking it; indeed it was difficult to get a word out of them in class. My Egyptian students had problems writing English but spoke it so well, and so continually, that I was waylaid going to and from class by students who just wanted to chat. In fact, they often surrounded me as soon as I left my apartment building and asked me questions about current events and about America until we were all late for class.

"What do you think of the hijacking of the Egyptian plane?" I'd hear from a voice beside me. I would explain that I didn't know about this because I didn't have a TV or a radio.

"Why is America so much more advanced than Egypt, when we have an older civilization?"

Dodging donkey carts and bicycles in the crowded street, I tried to explain something about rich natural resources and the work ethic.

"Do you like Michael Jackson?"

I said I thought he looked and sang like a girl, and I preferred men who looked like men.

"Isn't it true that black people suffer terribly in the United States?" There was a note of challenging superiority in this voice.

I pointed out that, being white, I was not in a position to know, but I'd be glad to lend him books by black American writers so he could judge for himself. That shut him up for the moment; he apparently did not actually want to read anything.

He was immediately superseded by a young man who wanted to know if I liked Egyptian men. Before I could answer that, a young woman in a headscarf wanted to know if all American women went to bed with men before they were married, or just some of them.

I felt as though I were a celebrity holding an impromptu press conference. In the evening, after my last afternoon class, the siege began again, only this time I was tired, gritty, and grumpy. This, despite the fears of well-meaning friends back home, was as close as I ever came to being taken hostage.

The classes were frequently a kind of tug of war. Thirty or forty of the students were genuinely interested in British poetry (although my grant and my specialization were in American fiction, British poetry was what I was asked to teach); these students, about half of them women, sat in the front four rows, took assiduous notes, and sometimes recorded the lectures on tape. The other fifty or so just wanted to learn to speak English well enough to get good jobs when they graduated and would frequently chat with each other during class or ask me totally unrelated questions about American society or foreign policy—the same sorts of questions I had already answered on the way to campus. They started asking these questions after I attempted the usual teacher's ploy of trying to shame them into silence by announcing that if they had something to say, they should share it with the rest of the class.

These students were also somewhat alarmed by the fact that I showed up for every class and kept them the entire class period. Their Egyptian teachers didn't do this, they told me. They were tired, they complained. Why didn't I just let them go? I told them that I wasn't tired at all and that I had no idea that young Egyptian men were so weak. This may have been the only dispute that I felt I clearly won. Or had I? When the class time was over and my blazer was covered with chalk from leaning up against the blackboard, they pounded me on the shoulders to "help me brush the chalk off my clothing." I couldn't help suspecting that their vigor was retributive.

Actually, they were fun. Rowdy, but fun. I certainly preferred the students who wanted to talk about Wordsworth's concept of childhood and the organic unity of the "Intimations of Immortality" ode, because I tend to find ideas more interesting than horseplay as well as more appropriate to a college classroom. But the others meant and did no harm. We simply didn't need one another's abilities. Instead of one literature professor, they needed a couple of friendly young male English as a Second Language (ESL) teachers who would argue politics with them in class and then play soccer with them when the class was over. Then I could teach the thirty or so students who were interested in literature without interruption or distraction. But this was not to be, except in the graduate courses.

The Egyptian educational system was much more at fault than the students were. Modeled on the British system, the curriculum took a chronological approach, beginning with Shakespeare and working its way up to Orwell and T. S. Eliot. Of course, this approach, reasonable for native speakers, overlooked the fact that most of the students had never read more than newspaper paragraphs of English in high school. Not surprisingly, they found Shakespeare incomprehensible. The best that most students could do, at least in the first year, was to read the plot summaries in Cliff's Notes.

And yet, by the time they had reached their third and fourth year, they could all speak English fairly well and write sentences that were comprehensible if not grammatically correct. And some of them could write correctly. Comparing this to my own dismal undergraduate attempts to learn French, I couldn't help admiring these students. They didn't have any language labs or libraries. Their professors missed many of their classes. The study of fiction consisted of memorizing plots, and the study of poetry of identifying metaphors and rhyme schemes. Yet they learned English, and some of them even liked literature.

They also came to class at considerable sacrifice. Most were not dormitory students, and unlike American commuter students, they didn't have cars. If they lived in Mansoura, they either walked or splurged twenty-five to fifty piasters for a taxi. This, I learned, was why so many of the women wore long skirts and headscarves—so they could walk the mile or so to campus without being harassed. Usually only the upper-class girls, whose parents had cars, would wear Western clothing. If they lived in the outlying villages, as many of them did, they had to take a series of inter-city taxis and then walk from the taxi station.

The reward for this sacrifice was that they would have a better chance of getting a job when they graduated. The beginning salaries they would get as teachers or government employees were fifty or so pounds a month, enough for clothes and pocket money if they continued to live with their parents, but not enough for the men to even think of marrying and starting families of their own. Nevertheless, most felt lucky to get even that, because unemployment in Egypt was about 30 percent. So I liked my students; whatever they lacked as students, they made up for in their abilities to make the best of prospects and conditions that would have driven most Americans to despair.

I felt much more ambivalent about many of the teachers I met. For one thing, their relationship with students seemed liked a form of class warfare. Most came from wealthy families and had been educated in Britain during the fifties, when the old wealthy families still retained many of their advantages despite Nasser's revolution. At least this was true of those who taught English. I had several complain to me that universities had declined ever since Nasser's reform had provided a free education for anyone who could pass the entrance exams.

"The universities are full of peasants now," one teacher complained to me. "How can you expect a peasant to understand Wordsworth?"

I pointed out that much of Wordsworth's work was about peasants, but my colleague was unfazed.

"About peasants, certainly," he said with a wave of the hand. "But surely not for peasants."

And yet . . . he was driving around to three different universities to try to support his family, actually showing up for most of his lectures, and he did read and publish. I was teaching these often ill-prepared students for one year; he would be teaching them for the rest of his life. And I'm not sure that the students suffered as much as one might suppose. True, one student had told me, "Our teachers don't want to teach us anything. They just scorn us for not knowing already," but she was in the minority. The rest seemed unaware that education could or should be any different, and it may have been the humanity mixed in the all the snobbery that made it so.

I recalled seeing a colleague having what looked like a very cordial conversation with a student; he welcomed him with a smile, patted him on the back, laughed; the student, who looked a bit nervous at first, was soon smiling too, although not as cheerfully. I couldn't follow most of the Arabic, but I could hear the student thanking the professor effusively as he left, I turned to the professor and asked him what all of that had been about.

"Oh, he was upset because I failed him and wanted me to change his grade, but I convinced him that was impossible and his best chance was to take the course again."

I still wish I knew exactly what he had said, and if the magic worked only in Egypt.

10

@@

Conversations with Adla

Adla was in a fix, although I'm sure it was not a major crisis for her. A large, pleasant-faced woman of about my age, she had many of the rewards of her society: the respect that came from being the wife of a doctor, the daughter of a wealthy old family, the mother of three attractive children, and an educated woman in her own right as well. She had a master's degree, taught one day a week in Mansoura, and was working on her Ph.D. The Ph.D. was the problem. She was interested in the New Critics, particularly Allan Tate. Her supervisor, who was also the chairman at Mansoura, knew little about Tate but much about the subject of his own dissertation, Sean O'Casey. Thus, he had assigned her the topic of applying Allan Tate's ideas about poetic tension to the writings of Sean O'Casey, little knowing that this was like asking someone to bake a cake while riding a bicycle. Under university rules, she could not change her topic without her supervisor's approval, which he was not about to give.

That was where I came in. They both hoped I could help her find some congruence between the two writers. I could not. But Adla and I became friends anyway, which not only assuaged my loneliness but gave me a look beneath the surface of Egyptian society into the world of the family, where people really lived.

Adla, like a growing number of Egyptian women, wore a long skirt and a headscarf when she went out in public, although her daughter Fawzia, a college student, did not. Zainab had hated wearing the *abayah* in Saudi Arabia and would no more have worn "Islamic clothing" in Egypt than would I. Adla also had far more traditional ideas about marriage and family than I did, or for that matter, than Zainab did. All of this made her different from Zainab and the other Egyptian women I had known and liked in Saudi Arabia and a new kind of person for me. And yet Adla had firm beliefs about women's strength of character and intellectual abilities. If I were to put her in a category, I would say she was a Muslim feminist, but that was still less than who she was.

Of course, at the same time that I was forming opinions about Adla and her society, she was forming opinions about me and mine, and her comments and questions were not always flattering. Frequently, I was irritated but interested, because she did give me an idea of how I seemed, as well as a sense of the dangers of assessing a society based on considerable reading and media viewing but few living examples.

"I've never known an American before," she told me repeatedly, "And you're not at all as I thought. You seem like just a normal person." *Saturday Night Fever* had been as big a hit in Egypt as in the United States; it was a central part of her image of modern America. She was apparently surprised to learn that middle-aged women college professors did not spend all their spare time in discos. (In fact, I had met many Arab women who had seen that movie on video and decided that if this was Western-style emancipation for women, they could do without it.) Of course, I had the advantage over her, because I had met other Egyptian women, my students and colleagues in Saudi Arabia, people like Zainab and her friends. But her comment did make me wonder if I was approaching Egyptian society with the same sorts of assumptions.

Other remarks hit closer to home.

"You know, you remind me of the American girl in that famous novel," she remarked to me one day as we sat in her kitchen. I was at the table chopping vegetables, because I had told her that if she wanted me to feel at home, she should give me some work to do. She looked back over her shoulder at me from the sink, where she was preparing a chicken. "You know, the one about the sweet little American girl who goes to Europe and scandalizes everyone by being too friendly to men." I had an idea what was coming, but I wasn't about to give her any help. I pretended that slicing cucumbers demanded my undivided attention.

"She knows she is breaking the conventions, but she has no idea what they mean," she added. "Ah. *Daisy Miller*. That's the name of the novel," she said triumphantly. It occurred to me, although apparently not to Adla, that ignorant ingenuousness might be far more attractive in an eighteen-year-old like Daisy than in a thirty-nine-year-old like me. I indignantly denied any resemblance, now slicing the cucumbers with great ferocity. Most annoying, there were ways in which she may have been right. Looking back at the snapshots of myself in Egypt, I see the bewildered and ingratiating smile of someone bumbling into the social conventions of another culture but hoping to be understood and excused anyway. Sometimes, indeed, I felt as though I had stepped into a nineteenth-century novel, and at other times, as though I had traveled back into the America of my own childhood. Perhaps I could have done better if I could have decided the exact time and place, or if Egypt had not seemed to be so many times and places intersecting and overlapping.

Appearances gave little clue. Heliopolis, the suburb of Cairo where Adla lived, was an upper-middle-class residential area with broad, straight streets, trees in courtyards and little parks, stores selling Western clothing and cosmetics, and ice cream and pastry shops where the young of Heliopolis ensconced and engorged themselves. Newer than Zamalek, it still didn't have the inhumanly shiny and chromey atmosphere of posh Western cities. It still felt like the America of the 1950s, like the sleepy Georgia and Carolina cities my family used to drive through on our way to Florida each winter. As I had then, I sensed both a calm and a tension beneath that calm.

Although Adla was fairly wealthy by Egyptian standards, her lifestyle was more like that of a lower-middle-class American. Adla's apartment building had that rarest of rare things, a functioning automatic elevator, and the three-bedroom apartment itself was roomy and pleasant. Most delightful, she had a large balcony shaded by a poinciana tree, where we later drank coffee while her two-year-old played with his toys. And yet, the walls of the apartment were cracked (the same shoddy construction that later caused so many buildings to collapse in the 1992 earthquake) and the water pressure in the plumbing was just enough to produce a moderate trickle. According to Adla, the first problem was caused by contractors bribing government inspectors to ignore violations and the second by thousands of squatters illegally tapping into the city water supply.

"But what do you expect them to do?" she said. "They can't live without water. The government thinks that if they don't give these people water and electricity, they'll stay in their villages, but they aren't going to do that as long as all the jobs are in Cairo." Her view of the government was echoed by almost every other Egyptian I talked to.

The difference between the building's outward modernity and

fashionable location and its inner construction flaws seemed emblematic of Egypt itself. To some degree, it seemed as if Egypt were just like Adla's building—on paper, a democracy, moderate, secular, Western-allied, but within, a corrupt dictatorship indifferent to the sufferings of its citizens. And I still think this is true.

But a more interesting truth was more multilayered, like Adla herself. And each layer was subject to differing interpretations, even on the most external level. To Westerners, her *hijab*, for instance, classified Adla as the oppressed victim of a patriarchal religion. To her society, on the other hand, it signaled that she was a respectable woman uninterested in attracting male attention. Both East and West tended to see the scarf as a barrier, shutting out unconventional thoughts or religious questioning, the East viewing this with acceptance, the West, with horror. Both superficial views discounted the fact that covering women's heads does not prevent them from thinking, as Adla and so many other Arab women showed me again and again. A Westerner wouldn't know this if she saw only the symbol and never thought to ask the person inside the symbol. From my students, I often got pat answers about religious convictions. If you wore a scarf, you had them. From Adla, I got a far more complex insight. She had not always worn the *hijab*. About ten years earlier, Adla had gotten fed up with transforming herself into a walking Barbie doll whenever she stepped out of the house and decided that Islamic dress was more dignified.

"I think it's more appropriate for a professor," she told me once, as we sat in the leafy courtyard of the Heliopolis Club, the sports club where she and other upper-middle-class Egyptians enjoyed a respite from Cairo's noise and crowds. "A man isn't going to take anything a woman says seriously if he is busy looking at her legs." Shortly after she spoke, a couple of young women walked by in tennis skirts and nobody paid them much attention, but I could still understand her point very well, especially because while she taught she would be standing in front of a class primarily composed of young unmarried men. In the States, I myself wore slacks so that I could sit informally on the edge of the desk without having to worry about students being able to see up my skirt. But it occurred to me slacks only worked to desexualize a woman in a society that had traditionally considered slacks men's clothing. The traditional Egyptian clothing for both men and women was a *gellabeyah*. Here slacks were considered Western and perhaps a bit sexy even for men, but doubly so for women.

As for the headscarf, of course, I knew the practical reason for covering one's hair in Egypt's dry, dusty, sunny climate. When I washed my hair at night, the rinse water looked like a farmer had just washed his buffalo in it, and my hair was turning into straw despite all the conditioners I slathered on it. In fact, when I went to Upper Egypt, I saw as many men with covered hair as I saw women. Over the past six thousand years, the Egyptians had figured out that it's not smart to walk around in the sun bareheaded. But of course, these practical reasons had nothing to do with the religious justifications. I knew that the Qur'an said nothing specifically about women covering their hair, so I was curious why Adla considered this a religious obligation when Zainab and other educated Muslim women did not.

Looking around the courtyard of the club, I could see an equal number of covered and uncovered heads. The fact that the covered heads usually belonged to women over thirty-five led me to speculate on a possible causal relationship between graying hair and Islamic modesty. Adla laughed, as she was getting a little gray at the temples herself, but then pointed out that if the problem were merely cosmetic, she and the others could just dye their hair like I did. (How did she know?)

"And the Qur'an does say," she pointed out gently, "that women should not display those parts of their bodies that are not normally in view. To me, this means that a woman who is wearing less clothing than the other women in her society is in danger of immodesty." Looking over at me, she hurried to add, "This might not be her intention, but this can be the effect. The majority of women in this country cover their hair, so it seems to me that I should too."

Yet if it were not for the scarves and the slightly more formal manners, we could have been at a country club in the States. It was the only place in Cairo or indeed in Egypt where I had seen so much grass and so many trees, and it occurred to me that this was the way the old aristocracy had lived fifty or sixty years ago, with huge gardens like this within the walls of their villas, each wealthy home an oasis amid the poverty and noise of the city. Now it was a place where the descendants of these old families, now merely upper middle class, could go sometimes on weekends and where they could send their children to play instead of having them play in the streets like the children of the poor. It was a remnant of privilege, like much of Adla's life.

Looking around at the other patrons of the club, we watched men and women in tennis clothes passing by on the sidewalk, children in bathing suits and teenagers with robes on over bathing suits, women veiled and unveiled walking arm-in-arm, Western-dressed and veiled teenagers sitting together eating ice cream at the tables near us. Perhaps this was even more tolerance of difference than in the United States. Across the courtyard, we could see a girl in a pastel headscarf drinking an orange soda with a young man who was drinking a beer, the two of them staring adoringly into each other's eyes the whole time.

"Of course," Adla continued, adjusting her scarf, "not all women feel as I do. Fawzia feels that as long as she doesn't dress provocatively (she was usually wearing slacks and a long overblouse when I saw her) she is not violating her religion. And everyone knows she is a well-brought-up, respectable girl. So I don't press her on this matter." She looked at the veiled girl with her beer-drinking boyfriend. "Obviously, behavior is more important than appearance in all moral issues, but it is better, I think, when moral appearance and moral behavior go together." As for the couple, she went on, they might be engaged; she made no moral judgement, but it was certainly inconsiderate of the boy to drink beer in public when he was with a girl who seemed to value moral appearance. "Thank God that girl isn't my daughter," she sighed. "I wouldn't want her to marry a boy like that."

I wasn't buying this argument. The concern with appearance seemed trivial to me, as did the tendency to equate morality so exclusively with sexual behavior. Besides, I tended to think that covering just created more curiosity. On the other hand, Adla had obviously thought about the idea of veiling and made a decision based on what gave her the greatest sense of control as she moved through her society. And she was not pushing her ideas on anyone else. It seemed to me that those Western pseudofeminists who would see her long skirt and headscarf and immediately classify her as brainwashed and unliberated were as narrow-minded as the Egyptian fundamentalists who classified women as immoral if they wore Western clothing. Busybodies who wanted to fix people they didn't even know, all of them.

Yet veiling, finally, was the least interesting of the things we talked about, perhaps because it was the most superficial difference between us. One evening, as we were walking together to the little grocery store near her apartment, she confided that a suitor had called to ask permission to court Fawzia. A brisk wind blew sand in our faces whenever we left the shelter of the buildings.

"I told him that she wanted to finish her education before she thought of such things. Actually, it's the fifth offer we have had, but we haven't told Fawzia about them. And she never asks. She's a good girl."

"What about after she graduates?" I wanted to know, digging through my purses for sunglasses, which would look pretty silly at this time of night but would at least keep the sand out of my eyes.

"Then her father and I will select the young men who seem the most suitable and introduce her to them. The choice will be up to her, of course."

We walked a few paces in silence. "Some of the students at Mansoura told me they were in love with boys in their class. What would you do if Fawzia were in love with one of her classmates?"

Having crossed the street, we were now in the shelter of the buildings again and I could listen with less distraction. "We are not old fashioned," she observed. "Her father and I would make inquiries about the boy and if he came from a good family and was respectable, we'd give our consent. In fact, that's how my husband and I married. It was a love match." Again I felt as though I were in a nineteenth-century novel, where a "love match" was something rare and romantic. Yet looking over at her, with her serene, well-formed face and measured walk, graceful despite her weight even now, I thought of how lovely Adla must have been as a young woman, and how she must have been sought after. I was happy for her that she had been able to marry for love. It was certainly much harder to do here.

As we walked on, I remembered something one of my students had told me about his sister, about how a young man had proposed to her but the family had pressured her to turn him down because the rest of the boy's family had a bad reputation. I had found this baffling and wondered if it were just my student's family who were a little odd, or if this was a general rule. Adla was someone I could ask. "What if he was all right but his family wasn't?"

Adla sighed. "This could be a problem. The boy might be very nice, but his family might expect us to do favors for them that might not be right to do, or they might try to involve our family in their quarrels. And what could we do then, when the man had our daughter living under his roof? Fawzia is a good girl, and she would do as we asked. But it might hurt her. I don't like to think about this."

It made a little more sense now, but it still struck me as sad. I was thinking about all of this when Adla remarked, "I've never understood about American mothers, how they could allow their daughters to marry just anyone, just because the girl is infatuated with him. How could a mother hand her daughter over to just anybody, not knowing who he is or what he has come from or how he would treat her daughter? It's hard for me to understand how a mother's feelings could be so different."

We turned the corner to the store in the dusty Cairo sunset, and I thought about that. Finally, I said, "I can't think of anything that would have made me more miserable than marrying a man my parents picked out for me. Even if there were nothing wrong with the man himself."

Adla was shocked. "We would never pressure Fawzia to marry a man she didn't like. That's inhuman. It's un-Islamic. We will try to make sure that the boys she meets are the right sort, that's all."

Both of us seemed to have missed the point. I remembered the Egyptian girls I had known in Saudi Arabia giving imitations of a nervous suitor calling on the family—spilling his tea, eagerly agreeing with the father's every opinion, all the while surreptitiously casting imploring glances at the giggling young lady. "They're all like Mr. Collins (Elizabeth Bennet's fatuous suitor) in *Pride and Prejudice*," one girl told me. "All of them. I don't know where my mother finds such men. She must ask all her friends, 'Do you have a donkey? If so, please send him over as a suitor for my daughter.' " Of course, in Egypt itself, young people could meet more freely, but the ultimate arbiter was still the family.

So while Adla was mulling over my last remark about the awfulness of having a parent-selected husband, I added, "And it seems to me that you can find out everything about a boy's family and still not know what kind of a person he is. The fact that he's polite in front of his fiancée's parents is no guarantee that the marriage is going to be happy."

"Nothing guarantees that a marriage will be happy," she said finally. "Does it? Not in any society. In America, everyone marries for love . . ." she looked at me questioningly, "isn't that right? And still more people end up getting divorced there than here."

She lowered her voice when she said "divorce," as though she were speaking of death. I felt then that I could never explain all the differences between our societies that made divorce not akin to death for American women, but sometimes even a kind of rebirth of an autonomous self. Looking at the world from within that network of family support and obligation, she was likely to hear in the term "autonomous self" something very different from what I meant. My students, after all, routinely understood "individualism" as a synonym for "selfishness," not because of their problems with English, but because they were unable to conceive of a society in which ones actions did not reflect on an entire family, or indeed in which everyone was not surrounded by an extended family and all the people with whom they had grown up. In a society where everyone of a certain class knows everyone else, "autonomous self" could only mean a very subtle and private thing. At any rate, it was easier to let it pass than to try to begin an explanation that might lead back to the stereotype of Americans as mean-spirited loners.

I have thought back over that conversation many times. Of course, what she said was true in many ways. Among my American friends, I only knew of a few marriages that seemed to be happy, and sometimes the people whom I had thought were so happy ended up divorcing. So much for telling about any human relationship from the outside.

Yet I met young Egyptians who were far from satisfied with their system. "I would like to marry a man who wants to marry me because I'm me, not because I'm from a good family and have a good reputation," one woman in her late twenties told me. Another time, a young man told me about his broken engagement. "She was young, well-educated, pretty, respectable, everything to make her suitable. I thought I could mold her thinking and make her into the sort of person I wanted, and she was entirely agreeable to this. But all she seemed to think about was the wedding and the household goods and the furniture. About everything else, from politics to films, she was happy to agree with everything I said. After a while, the idea of even talking to her began to depress me. I broke the engagement, although everyone blamed me for it."

When I told these stories to Adla on our way back from the store, she pursed her lips, which was as much disapproval as I ever saw her show toward anything. "I am glad he had the sense to break the engagement. I'm sure he would have made the poor girl very miserable if he had married her. I think I know the sort. He wants a girl to have her own ideas, but what would happen if she did disagree with him and could present her ideas very well? I don't think he would be happy."

In all the discussion of marriages, I sensed a preoccupation with appearance, with how the prospective spouse seemed to the outside world rather than who the couple were to one another. And, I pointed out to Adla more than once, although I had heard some young Egyptians complain about their system, I had never heard an American girl say, "I sure wish my mother would pick out a husband for me." Adla just laughed.

One time, again when we were having tea at the club, I pointed out to her how much her dissertation topics struck me as a bad arranged marriage. There she was, stuck with an unworkable topic because someone else thought it was "suitable," and as unable to change it for a better one as an unhappily married woman was to get a better husband. Or perhaps Tate and O'Casey themselves, coupled together into this impossible topic, were the bad marriage.

This struck her as amusing. "In this case, I want a divorce. Please, divorce me from Mr. Tate and Mr. O'Casey. Or let Mr. Tate marry Miss Dickinson, or some other poet I can apply his theories to."

I suppose because we could laugh together about these things, I felt more comfortable about trying out my theories of Egyptian society on her. Once, I suggested to Adla that it seemed to me that in Egypt, people accommodated themselves to fit into the institution of marriage, whereas in America, couples tended to redefine the institution to fit their needs.

"Every couple changes marriage around to fit their needs," she said, "here or anywhere."

And of course, it's hard to make accurate generalizations about marriage in any society. Adla and many of the other Egyptian women with whom I talked were convinced that wife-beating was virtually unknown in Egypt because the woman would always have her family to defend her if she were physically harmed. "Even if he's rude to her, if he shouts at her for no reason, her family would try to mediate and tell him to treat her more politely. So I can't imagine any family that would tolerate having their daughter beaten, unless the girl's family was very poor and the man's family was very powerful," she told me one day when we were sitting on her balcony drinking tea. "I've never heard any one speak of such a thing, and as you know, women do complain to each other about bad husbands."

But another woman, who did have an abusive husband, told me she never told her family about it because her father was old and she was afraid that if he confronted her husband, her husband would beat up her father too. I don't know how typical her situation was. There may well have been as much spouse abuse in Egypt as in America, or even more, with the lack of public discussion making it invisible. But I also can't help wondering how much the Western stereotype of Arab misogyny is a matter of projecting onto the Other the worst traits of our own culture. I thought of this in particular during an "ecumenical discussion" I listened to back in the States, which consisted mostly of Christian and Jewish pseudofeminists hectoring a lone Muslim male professor concerning Islam's alleged mistreatment of women. When the women triumphantly quoted a verse supposedly from the Qur'an (I was never able to find this quote) that said it was all right for a man to beat his wife as long as he did not actually injure her, I wished the Muslim had quoted to them the "spare the rod and spoil the child" verse from the Old Testament to "prove" with equal validity that Judaism and Christianity encouraged child abuse. You don't know much about a religion if you don't know how it resides within a society, I wanted to tell them. But more, I wondered what Adla would have said if she had been part of the discussion, and if the American women would have left the meeting as sure of their assumptions.

This is not to suggest that the situation of Egyptian women is ideal. Adla and I talked at length about how difficult it was for an Egyptian woman to get a divorce if her husband didn't initiate it—legal difficulties that Adla said were un-Islamic. We were again on her balcony, while her children were all at the club, allowing her to speak more freely. She had obviously thought about this matter a great deal. "There is a Hadith [saying of the Prophet] in which the Prophet tells a woman that she has the right to divorce her husband 'if she cannot bear the smell of his breath,' " she told me. "To me this means that Islam gives the woman a right to divorce, period. Why else would he have chosen such a frivolous example?" She looked out over the sunlit streets, lost in thought. "Divorce is not in a woman's own interest, unless the man is a total brute. A woman isn't going to want a divorce for a silly reason. It would be for a very good reason that she simply wouldn't want to talk about in public, that his immorality is in danger of corrupting their children, or something like that." I could not help wondering, at this point, what circumstances she had known, what women had confided in her, that made her take this tone when before she had seemed so shocked at the very idea of divorce. Perhaps she simply felt that she knew me well enough now to tell me her real feelings. "As the Egyptian law is now," she said with quiet anger in her voice, "if a woman needs a divorce, she has to be ready to get up in court and ruin the reputation of the father of her children. How many women would do that? The Prophet understood this very well, I'm sure." And I was beginning to understand how the Qur'an and the Hadith could be used to defend women's rights at least as convincingly as some Muslim men could use their interpretation of Islam to limit women's rights. The texts were at least as multilayered as Arab society itself, and that society was a hundred different cultures overlapping, coexisting, and changing.

When I thought back over all that Adla and other traditional Egyptian women had said, what I sensed, finally, were different expectations of marriage and of society. We Americans tend to expect our marriages to be happy and to be a major source of fulfillment in our lives. If they aren't we feel like failures, or we get divorces. Many of the Egyptian women I talked to merely hoped to be happy, and if they weren't, they tried to make the best of it, even if their husbands were unfaithful or they were simply very incompatible. On the other hand, they did expect society to provide some minimal protection. A woman could, in some cases, get her family to pressure her husband into giving her a divorce, as the Egyptian Nobel laureate Naguib Mahfouz repeatedly shows in his *Cairo Trilogy*. And so long as her own reputation was spotless, she could gather her children and go back to her parents' house, knowing that the community would blame her husband for mistreating her rather than blaming her for leaving. But this social protection evaporated if a woman's unconventional behavior led anyone to question her morals.

Adla admired women who put the stability of the family ahead of personal fulfillment. In many ways, her values seemed like those of many American women of a generation ago, as did her home. In fact, talking to her, even though we were about the same age, I kept feeling that I was arguing with my mother, which may have put me at a certain disadvantage. Still, I couldn't conclude that her values or ideas were wrong, exactly. The problem with both fifties America and present-day Egypt is that women may stay in destructive marriages not because of their values but because they have so little legal recourse. In fact, I'm not entirely sure one can separate traditional values from helplessness unless women have exactly the same legal and social rights as men. Remarkably, Adla agreed. But I would have to add that one of the social and legal rights most important to Adla was that women have the same rights as men to contest a divorce, not just to seek one.

I sometimes felt that learning about Egypt was for me what writing her dissertation was for Adla, going beyond what others had de-cided was simple and suitable into a world of baffling complexity. She had a topic that looked academically respectable—as long as one hadn't read Tate or O'Casey. The moment one read them with any understanding, the topic became ludicrous. In fact, it was an intellec-tual scandal. In the same way, most of the American media analyses and travel books about Egypt sounded perfectly sensible—until one actually became friends with Egyptians. So perhaps, it occurred to me, we Americans and our media-engendered images of the Arab world are another example of a bad arranged marriage.

11

Going Down to Upper Egypt

After I had been in Mansoura for a few months, I started making trips down to Upper Egypt, the southern part of Egypt that is also upstream from Cairo. This sounds like a contradiction in terms until you realize that the Nile, unlike most rivers, flows south to north. I had been hearing for months about the Saeed and the Saeedis, Upper Egypt and the Upper Egyptians. The Saeed was a primitive and exotic place, and Saeedis were both noble savages and the second most popular butt of Cairene jokes. In fact, every Egyptian joke I heard either began, "Mubarak was puzzled and said to his ministers . . ." or "There was a Saeedi boy who went to Cairo . . ." The salt of the earth, apparently, but not too bright and rather oversexed.

As soon as they heard that I was going to Upper Egypt with the department chairman to give a lecture (on American women writers) and to meet the graduate students he was supposedly supervising, my Mansoura students started warning me about Saeedi men. "They'll kidnap you," one boy warned. "Did you hear the joke about the Saeedis who tried to kidnap the belly dancer at the nightclub at the Nile Hilton?" And on he went, to explain how an enamored Saeedi had enlisted four of his friends to help him break into the nightclub in the middle of her act, fight off the crowd of hundreds of indignant patrons, and carry the struggling girl down to the waiting taxi, only to discover that not all of them could fit into it now that they had the dancer with them. "So they gave her ten piasters and told her she was going to have to take the bus," he declared triumphantly.

I told him I thought I could cope. (Actually, the joke may have been prophetic, although who carried off whom is a debatable point.)

The Saeedis themselves, I later learned, found these jokes about as amusing as Polish Americans did Polish jokes.

I didn't know what to expect, but the landscape did change almost as soon as the train was outside Cairo. Instead of green fields and villages as far as the eye could see, the green was limited to a narrow strip on one bank of the Nile. On the other side were desert cliffs. The towns and villages began to look poorer and dustier, although I would occasionally see a house with a brightly painted mural on one wall. I saw more camels and fewer donkeys and buffalo, more men in *gellabeyahs* and fewer in Western clothing, more farm women in black and fewer in the bright colors and pastels I had seen on women working in the fields in the Nile delta.

The people inside the train began to change as well. The people getting on the train were taller and thinner than most of the people in the delta. Apparently, the Saeed was the land of the tall, skinny people, which made me feel more comfortable. During my year in China, I'd felt like a giantess (at 5'7"), and even in Mansoura I was three or four inches taller than most of my women students. Here in the Saeed, only my hair, eyes, and skin color were odd.

I noticed that more of the businessmen in the first class section wore freshly pressed *gellabeyahs* instead of business suits—"more comfortable in the heat," the chairman explained to me—and almost the only women who did not have their hair covered also wore crosses around their necks. They were Coptic Christians. Yet no one stared at them when they moved around the railway car, nor did they seem particularly intimidated. Perhaps the Saeedis were more sophisticated than I had been led to believe.

Some fourteen hours later, we arrived in Qena, the Upper Egyptian city that was to be a center of clashes between Islamists and the Egyptian government in 1988 and again in 1992. A group of four or five young teachers was waiting on the railway platform to meet us, but I was in no humor to be cordial. Not only was I dusty and sweaty, I had also had to put up with the chairman for this ungodly length of time. Much to my embarrassment, he had wanted to discuss D. H. Lawrence's sex life and the scenes that had most shocked him from the Ken Russell film of Lawrence's *Women In Love*. Apparently they shocked him so much that he had seen the film several times and memorized every scene that offended him, because he described them in great detail and with great animation. In theory, he wanted to discuss Lawrence because one of his Upper Egyptian graduate students was writing his master's thesis on him; in fact, he seemed to want me to confirm his own theory, based on seeing the film and hearing bits of literary gossip, that any man who would write about sexuality in such detail must be either impotent or homosexual. I did not concur, but on the other hand, there is a level of stupidity with which it is useless to argue. In exasperation, I finally tried looking out the window and answering in monosyllables. In retaliation, he gave me two rough drafts of master's theses to read, one on Lawrence and one on Oscar Wilde. He didn't have time to read them, he told me, and went to sleep. In my frustration and suppressed wrath, I wrote tart comments on the margins of the drastically oversimplified but otherwise innocuous theses.

This was part of the reason that I was somewhat embarrassed to learn that the two courteous young men waiting for us on the platform were the authors of the theses I had just commented upon. The other reason was that this was normally their day off, and they had just spent it trying to round up students to attend the lecture I was supposed to give that evening. It was a weekend, and most of the students were home in their villages with their families. The chairman had not thought to tell me that before. Nor did he tell me that my lecture had been officially scheduled to begin about a half-hour before we had arrived.

Never did I feel in such contrast with my surroundings. The sun was setting over cliffs on the opposite bank of the Nile, bathing the railway platform in rosy light. Two well-dressed young ladies and two young men in coats and ties were welcoming me and asking me polite questions about my trip. I wanted to look over the notes for my lecture, take a bath, and then, if there was time left over and I still felt so inclined, hit the chairman over the head with a large heavy object. Nothing went as planned and no one seemed to mind except me, probably because I was the only one who expected that anything would go as planned. When I said I wanted to wash up before I gave my lecture (I meant I wanted to be taken to where I was going to stay so that I could take a bath), one of the women escorted me to the women's rest room, where I splashed some cold water on my face. The rest of me remained as dusty and smelly as before.

The lecture proved not to be so bad after all. Eighty or so attentive students sat in the front rows of a spacious lecture hall that looked something like a high school auditorium back home. That is, it had seats instead of wooden benches and lighting that worked, both an improvement over Mansoura. Afterward, they asked intelligent questions, silly questions, and in-between question, all with the same poise and good humor. One young woman was puzzled by the idea of feminist rage, I recall. What good did it do to get so angry, she wanted to know. You just made yourself miserable and antagonized everyone else so that you never got what you wanted.

Under ordinary circumstances, I could probably have taken that as advice for dealing with my visit to the Saeed as well. But it was now 9:30 P.M.; I had been up since five that morning; I still had had no bath; I would be staying, I learned, in the women's guest house, which had no hot running water; and the graduate students whose theses I had commented upon wanted to speak with me a moment so that I could clarify some of my remarks. They had also ordered dinner for all of us at a restaurant, where we would be eating at around eleven o'clock. As it turned out, we ate around twelve-thirty, because the restaurant owner wasn't sure we were really coming, so he didn't start cooking until he saw us.

And yet, there were enough compensating factors that if I had only been able to have a bath and a nap, it would have been a lovely evening. We were accompanied by a very nice American ESL teacher named George, who expressed sympathy with my exhaustion and commented that it was hard to be nice to people who are being nice to you when you are so tired you are ready to drop. Egyptians normally take long afternoon naps during the heat of the day, so it hadn't occurred to anyone else that midnight might be past the bedtime of any normal-looking adult. He also told me that Mamoun, the teacher writing the thesis on Oscar Wilde, had suggested that, as George had an extra bedroom and hot running water, I might be more comfortable staying with him.

"I was going to offer, but I didn't want to destroy your reputation," he told me. "But I figured that if someone local suggested it, there shouldn't be any problem."

I looked gratefully at the young man in question and deeply regretted having written "So what?" beside observations in his thesis that had struck me as overly obvious.

It was a beautiful evening, starry and just slightly cool, with a light breeze rustling through the palm trees overhead. When the food arrived, I began to get my second wind, or else I was too delirious with exhaustion to feel tired any more. Or perhaps it was the company. The young teachers asked me far more intelligent and sophisticated questions about Lawrence and Wilde than I had expected to hear: both wanted to know what aspects of British society the writers were rebelling against, and how what I had seen of Egyptian society seemed to embody the same problems. Then they told me what they thought, namely, that Egyptian society was Victorian society without the industrial revolution. "Only warmer," Salem, the man writing on Lawrence, added.

I think he was right; all the joking, all the physical and emotional touching between people of the same sex did seem very un-Victorian. But perhaps, I thought to myself, the real Victorians were different from the popular image of them. After all, just about everything else I had been told had been proven wrong. I had been told in America that I was going to a violent culture and found myself in a country where passersby intervened to prevent any public dispute from turning into a fistfight. I had been told in Mansoura and Cairo that the Saeedis were backward and I was now talking to the most sophisticated Egyptians I had met. In fact, for the first time since I had come to Egypt, I was talking to people who were using the literature of another culture to better understand their own. So perhaps the Victorians hadn't been so Victorian after all.

As the night progressed, I learned that these graduate students also wanted to know something else. Was I going back to Cairo in the morning on the train with the chairman, or could I stay the day with them, take in the pharonic temple of Hathor at Dendara, and give a talk to one of their classes about Hemingway and Lawrence? Then I could take the half-hour flight back to Cairo in the evening. It wasn't a difficult choice.

Dendara

When I was about twelve, I read H. G. Wells's *The Time Machine,* and thereafter it was a central part of my literary daydreams. I read about Vikings, and imagined finding a lost Viking, brought hither by the time machine, wandering in the woods in back of my house and in need of being brought up-to-date about the world by me. A few years later, when I read Byron's poems and developed the same crush on him as the ladies of his day had, I traveled back to the nineteenth century to meet him. But the constant was the ancient Egyptians. Every time I quarreled with one of my friends or my contemporaries on the school bus teased me for reading too much, I would be off to ancient Egypt: magical, peaceful, sun-burnished. And now, this morning I really was off to ancient Egypt.

At the school, the two young women were waiting for me with a car. Although in the exhaustion of the evening before, they been a blur of nicely dressed propriety, I could see now that they were quite different: Fatma, angular, dark complected, and in her early thirties, and Alia about ten years younger, with a pretty face and an ironic sense of humor. It was she, I recall, who asked me with a certain archness how I had slept. "Like the dead," I said, which seemed to startle them. To cover their discomposure, they apologized in advance for the temple. It was actually not very old—Ptolemaic rather than Middle Kingdom like the temples at Luxor. There was another temple underneath it, but it could not be excavated without destroying the Dendara temple. What I would be seeing was only a little over two thousand years old.

I told them about visiting the Chinese art exhibition in Washington with Hala, my Egyptian student from Saudi Arabia. Looking at T'ang dynasty paintings, I had marveled at the fact that what we were seeing was a thousand years old.

"Ah," Hala had said. "Very recent."

Still, as we got out of the car and I got my first look, I did feel slightly disappointed. It somehow did not look two thousand years old. But that, I realized later, was partly because it wasn't a ruin. The Parthenon and the Colosseum felt old because they were crumbling— and because I had seen the image of those ruins in art history textbooks all my life. I had never seen the Dendara temple before, only images from unidentified tomb paintings of people plowing fields or baking bread. The gentleness of those images, I think, had been what had attracted me so long ago, and there was none of that in the massive stone building in front of me. The awe that it should have evoked is perhaps something learned.

At the door of the temple, between two huge pillars, sat an old man in a full, blue *gellabeyah* and a jauntily tied wool turban, the end dangling rakishly over his ear. He was the security guard, and he would show us through the temple. I had seen people dressed as he was from the window of the train, but they had seemed then simultaneously to be part of the landscape and people from another time, people I could see but not speak to, like illustrations in books. Then with a start I realized why that was. They looked like the people in the illustrated Bible stories I had read as a child. Seeing the guard face-to-face, even though I could only speak to him through Fatma and Alia, was a double time trip—to a Biblical past and to my own childhood.

What did it mean to these young women, I wondered, to be living next to three or four thousand years of history? Did they feel connected to it? Later, when we were in the temple, I asked them.

"Of course. We are Egyptians, and this is Egypt's heritage," the older woman, Fatma, responded.

But Alia, the younger, wasn't so sure. "Personally, no," she said frankly. "It's too far from my life. In a way, your culture seems closer to me, even though I've never been to your country. And this is a great pity, I think. Because as you can see, it's very beautiful." She pointed to the carving of the head of Hathor, the goddess of love and fertility, on top of one of the pillars. It was a round-cheeked human face with a cow's ears and horns. On the face was a strange half-smile, the same haunting smile I had seen on the faces of Archaic Greek statues in the museum in Athens. Yet this seemed more alien.

As if on cue, the security guard who was escorting us pointed to the sculpture of Hathor and laughed. "Hosni Mubarak," I heard him say clearly.

I knew well these bovine jokes about Mubarak. In Cairo there was a popular French brand of cream cheese, *La vache qui rit*, whose logo was a fat red cow with a sly smirk on her face. (I always figured she was laughing because she had tricked me into buying the French version of Cheez Whiz.) At any rate, this logo was alleged to resemble the president. When talking politics, Egyptians I knew would simply say "La vache qui rit" if they didn't want to mention Mubarak by name.

I wondered why it was that the easiest way to respond to these beautiful, remote images was to make jokes about the present. Looking at the tomb paintings at Sakara, I had heard other Americans making the same kinds of jokes—that the food-laden bearers were insistent Egyptian hostesses pressing still more rice and lentils on their stuffed guests, while the odd palms outward gestures of the seated figures were those same guests signaling, "Couldn't eat another bite." It seemed so funny, I supposed, because all we had was the solemnity of the faces and gestures without their meaning. It was picture stripped of sound and intelligibility, funny in the way that silent movies seem funny. Yet there was the sheer beauty of the images themselves, the half-smiles, the intricate gestures of the long and delicate hands, the perfectly proportioned bodies in loincloths or transparent robes. The mystery of that beauty was powerful and discomforting, so we laughed to make ourselves feel connected to our own world again.

The power of that beauty had certainly evoked a real hostility in the past. Almost all the frescoes on the ceilings had been destroyed by fires set by early Christians determined to erase these images of the pagan past. It happened here, I guessed, rather than in Greece, because here the images still had a real power and because they so clearly represented something superhuman, nonhuman, human and animal, human and god. Something in people wanted to destroy what was beautiful, vital, and alien in the past, whether through vandalism or laughter. I wondered if there was something of this in America's antagonism toward the Middle East. I looked again at the old security guard, dressed like one of the wise men in a Christmas pageant in his long blue robe and turban, yet separated from my culture by language and belief. He was the kind of colorful native that appeared in so many travel books, laughed at perhaps because of his very connection to a living past, a vital but seemingly alien culture. I looked over at Fatma and Alia, who spoke my language so well and dressed so much like I did that I could forget that they and the old man shared that same language and belief. Alia and Fatma were too pretty and modern-looking and articulate to laugh at, which may be why people like them never seemed to appear in American travel books or news reports. I wondered about those early Christians, destroying all the images of beautiful alien paganness they could find, never realizing that they had destroyed a part of themselves along with them.

We moved into one of the rooms undamaged by fire, the old man in his *gellabeyah* leading us like an Old Testament prophet, we ladies dressed as if for an afternoon tea, in pumps and skirts and earrings, following. It was then that I realized another of the pasts of time and place that I had walked into. Looking at Fatma and Alia, I realized that the strange semi-Western nostalgia I had sensed from Western-dressed Egyptians was not for an America of the 1950s, as I had so often felt, but an England of the 1950s that I too only knew about from books and movies. For them, it was a frozen colonial past. When Alia had said she felt closer to "my culture" than the pharonic past, she did not mean the culture of contemporary America. She meant the version of British culture she had learned from her parents and of which speaking English had reminded her.

Above our heads was a figure that dwarfed such thoughts for a moment, a huge elongated figure of a woman with her weight on her hands and feet, a sun disc in her mouth and another sun disc springing from her vagina. This was the goddess Nut giving birth to the universe, an elegantly stylized image of the strain of creation. How different, I thought, from the passive female nudes of Western art.

"What do you think of it?" I asked Fatma, whose face, I realized, was very like that of the goddess over our heads—the olive skin, the high cheekbones, the large strangely set brown eyes.

"It's breathtaking, of course," she said.

"It may be breathtaking," Alia remarked, "but when my time comes, I want a hospital and very good doctor."

I sympathized but suddenly found myself picturing Nut in a hospital gown surrounded by doctors and nurses. It was no use. I could not simultaneously appreciate the company of these witty young women and the splendors of pharonic art; the time machine was rocketing back and forth between too many centuries. I opted for the present, and we talked a little about graduate study. The old security guard, seeming more relaxed now too, occasionally pointed out some two-thousand-year-old image on the wall but seemed more concerned with locating his matches in the pockets of his *gellabeyah*.

When we were outside, I turned and looked back at the temple, standing there by itself in the desert, the same weathered beige as the desert, as if it were an expression of the desert itself. It wasn't like a Greek temple; it wasn't something I had been taught to see as a marvel of ancient art and engineering. It was heavier, more solid, more absolutely undeniable. It said there was a world different from my own, and that world was not dead, decayed, or buried, no matter what we said or failed to say. The sky arched above it cloudless blue, the guard was now a splash of blue in the doorway, and we were tiny spots of color moving away from its static splendor, moving back toward the normality of our lives.

12

Escaping the Tribe

> But he heard high up in the air
> A piper piping away,
> And never was piping so sad,
> And never was piping so gay.
> —"The Host of the Air," W. B. Yeats

I was moving through different worlds, as I suppose we all do to differing degrees. I was moving among the Egyptian universities, the Americanized Egypt of my fellow Fulbrighters, the tourist hotels of Cairo, and the library of the American University in Cairo. Salem and Mamoun, the Upper Egyptian teachers, were moving among the worlds of modern Cairo, tribal Upper Egypt, and Western literature. We were all moving through one world and trying to escape into another, leaving pieces of ourselves behind with each partial escape. I came back to my own world. Mamoun, whom I married a little over a year later, escaped into my world, becoming something like an American but never ceasing to be an Arab, an Egyptian, and a Saeedi. Salem fell in between these worlds in yet another way.

It had been settled. Mamoun and Salem would travel to Cairo every two or three weeks so that I could help them revise their theses. For me, it meant a two-hour bus ride from Mansoura and staying at the Fulbright flat. For Mamoun and Salem, it meant a thirteen-hour train trip and staying with Mamoun's younger brother, a medical student, in his tiny apartment near Al Azhar, Cairo's Islamic university. Helping them with their theses assuaged some of my original guilt about the unpleasant comments I had written in their margins, but both were so nice to me that the original guilt was replaced by a new one: the long, miserable trip they were making for the sake of my assistance. I agreed to travel again to Upper Egypt, stay again in

George's apartment (although he was away, he gave me the key), and spend the weekend discussing their work.

From meeting both young men in Cairo, I had gotten to know something about them. Mamoun had spent the previous summer at Georgetown University in Washington as a graduate Fulbright student. He was also a short-story writer and a poet, occasionally publishing his work in one of the big Cairo dailies, *al-Akhbar* (The News). (I had been wondering how Egyptians got a chance to read anything literary, because most of the libraries I had seen were wretched, and books were expensive for anyone trying to live on an Egyptian teacher's salary.) We had talked about culture shock, his and mine. For him, the greatest shock had not been going from Cairo to Washington, but from Upper Egypt to Cairo.

Sitting in a coffee shop near the American University, he told me that his village in Upper Egypt had been without electricity and running water until he went away to college and had only now gotten its first doctor. Before, sick people had to travel by donkey to a clinic ten miles away. His parents wore the traditional *gellabeyahs* of Upper Egypt, his mother dressing all in black with only her face, hands, and feet showing, his father equally covered but dressed in lighter colors. "And when I go back to the village, that's how I dress too." he told me.

I looked at this sophisticated man, now dressed in black slacks and a white cotton shirt and carrying a Georgetown backpack, and tried to imagine him wearing a *gellabeyah* and turban like the security guard at Dendara. With his Turkish coffee in one hand and his cigarette in the other, he looked as darkly handsome and interestingly complicated as the romantic lead in some fifties French film. I could not picture him in a *gellabeyah* riding a donkey. And yet that too was part of who he was.

When Mamoun's first story was accepted, the literary editor of *al-Akhbar* had invited him to Cairo to meet him in the coffee shop of the Nile Hilton, a glass-and-steel high rise.

"I just stood there gaping in astonishment," he told me. "I'd never seen an elevator before, or wall-to-wall carpeting. I was afraid every minute that the doorman would realize that I was really just a Saeedi farm boy and throw me out."

And Cairo itself was shocking: women driving cars, women smoking and wearing miniskirts, Egyptian men and women sitting together in cafés just like Western tourists, the noise and the traffic, the strange

Cairo accent, and the growing realization that his own accent sounded amusingly backward to the Cairenes.

That had been five years ago. After that, Washington had been just a change of scene. Well, not exactly—he had been surprised about many things, but they were of a different order. We found a great deal to talk about, and it was he who helped me to understand what was happening to Salem.

After a couple of meetings in Cairo during which we had discussed D. H. Lawrence's ideas about love, Salem had confided in me. He himself had a problem. Salem too was a handsome man, looking rather like a young Harry Belafonte, except perhaps slightly lighter and decidedly shorter. (Indeed, many Egyptians look like light-skinned African Americans.) He was in love with a girl and she loved him, but her parents objected to the marriage. Following Egyptian tradition, he had gone to the girl's father to ask permission to marry her. The father had told him politely that the family had no objection to him personally, but unfortunately, they didn't marry outside their tribe. He was thinking about marrying her anyway. What did I think he should do? Knowing nothing about the traditions of Upper Egypt or why this particular family didn't want to marry outside the tribe, I assumed that the problem was merely of social disapprobation, which, of course, Lawrence thought that lovers should flout. I myself wasn't quite as sure as Lawrence; after reading his biographies, it seemed to me that his wife had paid a higher price than he had imagined (estrangement from her children) and that estrangement from her parents could affect an Egyptian girl in much the same way.

"She is willing to pay that price," he told me.

I shrugged. Why not, then. I couldn't imagine anything much worse than not marrying someone you loved because of social criticism and then later marrying someone else who was merely "suitable." As he was in his mid-twenties, he surely ought to know whether or not he was in love and what the social consequences would be of marrying a woman without her family's consent. And because they were both Muslims, it never occurred to me that the problems could entail more than having to deal with gossip and angry parents.

Later, I began to wonder why he had asked me, when I obviously understood nothing of the true dimensions of his dilemma. I supposed, finally, it was because only I could give him the answer he wanted to hear.

Both Salem and Mamoun were waiting for me when I arrived at the airport in Luxor, a tourist city about thirty miles from Qena. Actually, the two of them had been happily watching the Africa Cup soccer match on the TV in one of the airport employee's offices. To the great jubilation of all the Egyptians in the airport, Egypt had won.

Later, when we had found a taxi and were speeding over bumpy blacktop roads back to Qena, I was curious about why it had taken two of them to fetch me. After all, one of them could easily have stayed home to watch the game without interruption.

"We can't let this little fellow (Salem was about five-foot-five and did not seem particularly pleased at being referred to that way) go around by himself these days," Mamoun told me. Taking turns, they explained to me what had happened. After Salem had asked to marry the girl, Aisha, her family had begun to pressure her to marry someone else, someone from her tribe. Not only did Aisha refuse to leave her room to meet her suitors, she ran away from home and had shown up at Salem's parents house a few days before.

"She's a very strong-minded girl," Salem broke in enthusiastically.

But of course, whatever this strong-minded girl's plans may have been, she couldn't stay. Even chaperoned by Salem's parents, she couldn't stay in the house, and nobody except Aisha herself had thought it was a good idea for Salem to marry her on the spot. If he did, her family might have killed them both, and Salem's parents along with them.

Riding along with the two of them, it seemed as if they were telling me the plot of a novel, not something that had actually happened. I couldn't put this violent love story together with the passing scenery, the sunny weather, and the excitement over the soccer win. And I couldn't associate the threat of tribal violence with either of these poised, articulate men, or indeed with any of the Egyptians I had met. Salem, sitting in the front seat next to the driver, smoking a cigarette, and turning around to add comments whenever Mamoun left something out of the story, seemed remarkably cheerful for a man whose life had been recently threatened, so I found it difficult to really believe that it had been. I didn't doubt what they told me, and yet it didn't feel true. Perhaps telling it as they did was a way of making it feel untrue to them as well.

Salem took over the narration at this point, recounting the events with polish and flair. Realizing that Aisha was not going to go home of her own accord, he told her that they would elope to Cairo and be married there, where at least his parents wouldn't be involved. She agreed, they got into an intercity taxi, and Salem paid the driver an extra five pounds to take them to Aisha's village instead, where he left her off in front of her house. At first, she didn't want to get out of the taxi, but when her family spotted her, she really didn't have any choice.

"Then I left very fast," Salem said with a laugh. "The Peugeot is an excellent car. Very good acceleration." Later, back at George's apartment, as they watched the soccer awards while I showered and changed, I heard them talking in worried voices.

"I was just telling Salem," Mamoun explained to me, "that he should perhaps stick around us this weekend. You're a foreigner, and I come from a big family, so they can't risk taking a shot at him and getting one of us by mistake. You wouldn't be in any danger, but I thought that you should still decide."

Thinking it was all very exciting, I quickly agreed. Talking to Mamoun about it later, I tried to understand. It was not about race or skin color. Egyptians have been a mixture of Hamitic and Semitic peoples since the time of the pharaohs and the skin colors range from pale ivory to dark brown without anyone seeming to give it much thought. Nor was it about money, exactly, because all of them were poor villagers, Aisha's family only a little more prosperous than Salem's. Besides, as a college teacher, he certainly had better prospects than a farmer. It was lineage. Aisha's family were *Ashraf*, people who claimed descent from the Prophet; Mamoun's family were tribal Arabs, people who traced their ancestry back to specific villages in central Arabia. This was a rung below the *Ashraf*. Beneath them were the *fellaheen*, the native Egyptians, and at the bottom of the hierarchy, the *Jamasa*, a tribe that had once been water carriers, apparently a lowly occupation. Salem was a *Jamasa*. It was not a caste system, exactly, because the only discrimination concerned intermarriage, and then only when a woman wanted to marry a man from a lower tribe. Nevertheless, the local notables, the *'omdahs*, tended to be *Ashraf* and tribal Arabs, and not being able to intermarry with them kept the *fellaheen* and *Jamasa* out of traditional positions of authority.

I tried to think of an American equivalent and could not. It wasn't like an interracial marriage, because the family could receive Salem cordially and tell him he was a fine young man to whom they had no objection personally—and then feel honor-bound to kill him if he persisted, not out of rage but out of duty. Worse, they would have had to kill their own daughter as well, or the entire extended family would be permanently disgraced.

We spent the rest of the afternoon and early evening at the college, a relatively safe place for Salem as well as a pleasant place to discuss what they had been writing. Their office, which they shared with two other young teachers, was considerably larger and more comfortable than offices I had been assigned in my early days of teaching and had a lovely view of a garden below. In fact, the liberal arts department building was an old mansion, a graceful edifice with a huge double staircase and a domed roof, unlike any other college building I had ever seen. I learned later that it had been one of the winter residences of King Farouk. The thick-walled upstairs rooms that were now offices had probably once been bedrooms, and even in the afternoon heat, the whole building stayed cool. However, there were no screens on the windows and by dusk, we were invaded by mosquitoes the size of hummingbirds, all of whom seemed to think that I had come to Qena for the purpose of feeding them.

Well after dark, we ventured out in search of something to eat. At that time, Qena seemed to have two modes of transportation, horse-drawn carriages and feet. Both were a great delight to me. The carriages were not there for tourists (who usually skipped Dendara to go straight to the older temples of Luxor) but for the locals, allowing me to enjoy the ride without feeling like a tourist. And walking was pleasant because the presence of Mamoun and Salem deterred unsolicited comments on my appearance.

It was fun, walking though the winding half-lit streets, the occasional fruit-seller's cart illuminated by candles, girls in long skirts and headscarves walking arm-in-arm, window-shopping, men in *gellabey-ahs* chatting in cafés. Like every Arab city I had seen, Qena was most alive at night. The air was full of the smell of charcoal, roasting meat, and *sheesha,* the strong tobacco Egyptians smoke out of water pipes. In the distance, we could hear drums and cymbals and the sound of *zaghrouta.*

We bought kebab and salad from an open-air restaurant and then took it to a park beside the Nile to eat. The park was closed, but the chain on the gate allowed it to open far enough for a thin person to pass through. We ranged from very thin (Salem) to reasonably trim (me), so we had no problem. Mamoun joked that the gate was designed only to keep out Northern Egyptians, a much stockier folk than the Saeedis. Indeed, the old groundskeeper, who came over to check what we were doing, was quickly mollified with a small tip, which I thought of as an entrance fee to make myself feel less guilty about trespassing.

It was lovely. We could hear the Nile and feel the evening breeze, which was just slightly cool. The wind rustled the palm fronds over-head, and the moonlight illuminated every shrub and flower. I could see Salem and Mamoun's faces clearly, and neither of them looked very worried.

"You really aren't in much danger, are you?" I ventured, helping myself to some of the kebab.

"I'm not," Mamoun said cheerfully. "I'm just a colleague of the miscreant. And besides, I come from a big tribe and they couldn't do anything to me without starting a feud. And you're not, of course, because you're a *khawaga* and they wouldn't want to hurt a foreigner. But that little guy over there, he has a big problem."

Salem laughed feebly and then declared, "But I am going to marry her, you know. Not right away, of course. But I'll find a way to get a scholarship to the States the way you did and take her there with me."

Mamoun laughed. "That's an example of his problem right there," he pointed out. "Advanced stupidity. But he's probably all right for now unless Aisha runs away again. Then they'll be sure that she and Salem are planning to elope."

Again, they were so lighthearted about it that it seemed as if it were happening to someone else, with the vague assurance that all would somehow end happily. Nevertheless, Salem's plan of escaping to the United States did not strike me as very realistic. I speculated aloud about how much D. H. Lawrence had to do with this. Was this another example of a conflict of cultures?

No, they told me, Arab girls didn't have to read D. H. Lawrence to want to elope with men their families wouldn't let them marry. Arabic literature was full of such star-crossed lovers. Nor was Aisha particularly unusual. Upper Egypt, they told me, was full of such Romeos and Juliets.

"And generally, they end up as dead Romeos and Juliets," Ma-moun pointed out.

I couldn't help wondering where the police were in all of this. Surely all of this must be against the law. And indeed it was against both Islamic law and national law. The actual murderer in these honor killings was usually arrested and sent to prison. But the killer was still a hero in the eyes of most of the villagers, and the honor of the family was still preserved. Until there came a time when the villagers considered it more shameful to go to prison than to allow a woman to marry outside the tribe, there was little the government could do to stop the practice.

And the system of vendettas and blood feuds was so entrenched that the central government was helpless to stop it. Yet that implied that the government was more civilized than the villagers, when the questions were far murkier. Sitting in the grass with the moonlight reflecting off the Nile, Mamoun told me the story of what had happened in his village when he was a child.

The central government had decided to merge two small villages —or neighborhoods: it was difficult for outsiders to tell where one village ended and the other began. To the villagers themselves, however, it was very clear. One village was composed of one subtribe of tribal Arabs, the other village of a different subtribe. When the government appointed an *'omdah,* or mayor, from one tribe, the other tribe felt so aggrieved that one of their tribesmen shot the *'omdah* as he was crossing the Nile in a boat. The *'omdah'*s tribe retaliated, not against the actual killer, who had been carefully smuggled out of the region so that he wouldn't be arrested, but by killing one of the other tribe's most prominent citizens. Again, that tribe retaliated. Then the army moved in and imposed a curfew.

"Nobody could go out of his house, even to get food. When my father tried to leave the house to buy bread, a soldier hit him with a rifle butt." Mamoun told me, suddenly serious now. "I'll never forget how shocked and hurt I was, to see my father hit like that. And he couldn't do anything to defend himself because the soldier had a gun and there was nothing to stop the soldier from shooting."

Eventually, the villages were redivided, and an *'omdah* appointed from each village's clan. But none of it would have happened in the first place, Mamoun pointed out, if the villagers had been able to elect their own *'omdah* rather than having him appointed by the central government. The government had the outward trappings of modern thought and an authoritarian mentality underneath. No wonder the villagers resisted it. In fact, they all seemed to ignore the Cairo government most of the time. Nobody ever went to the police about thefts of farm animals or the other property crimes that were common enough, and other disputes were resolved through informal mediation rather than the courts.

To relieve the somber atmosphere, Mamoun then told another story, very different in tone, about a family living in a nearby village who had tried to steal his family's cow. "But my cousin happened to be looking out the window and saw them leading the cow out of the shed—it was a moonlit night like tonight—and told her father about it. There were only two ways that the thieves could get back to their house, both by crossing bridges. So my uncles and cousins and brothers all got rifles—or sticks that would look like rifles in the dark—and sat on each of the bridges for the rest of the night. What could the thieves do? They had the cow, but they couldn't get home with her and everyone in our village knew the cow was ours. All night, they walked back and forth between the two bridges. I don't know what was in their heads. Maybe they kept hoping that they had just imagined a group of armed men sitting on the other bridge," he laughed. "Or maybe they thought we would get bored and go away."

"Wasn't it boring to sit on the bridge?" I asked.

"Not nearly as boring as walking back and forth with a cow all night was for the thieves," Salem added.

"At any rate, just before the dawn prayer they gave up and turned the cow loose, and she went home on her own. But I couldn't resist saying something to their son the next day at school. I said, 'I saw the strangest thing when I looked out the window last night. Your father was leading our cow round and round the village, like some rich foreigner walking his dog.' He just said, 'Yes, some cow got loose and strayed to our village and we were trying to find the owner.' "

We all laughed, although it occurred to me later that perhaps there was a larger significance in the story, something about the Egyptian way of resolving conflict or perhaps about a more universal dilemma of feeling besieged and unable to escape. Yet sitting there in the grass listening to these stories, I couldn't help finding all they told me exotic and charming and exciting, even the story about Salem and Aisha. The narratives all blurred together in the moonlight, now and long ago, storyteller's suspense and real danger. And I suppose that was what they both wanted me to feel.

But it was getting late, the mosquitoes had figured out where I had moved, and people who don't take afternoon naps get grumpy when kept up past midnight. They walked me back to George's apartment through the silent streets.

The next morning, after I gave a lecture and visited with Alia, the young woman teacher, the two men went with me in a taxi to the airport in Luxor. The plan was for me to spend a few hours sightseeing and then catch my plane. Along the way, they joked as usual. We stopped briefly outside Salem's village, a cluster of adobe houses next to a canal, while he scrawled a note which he gave to a boy on a bicycle.

"What's that all about?" I asked.

"I don't know," Mamoun said stonily.

A few miles later, our way was blocked by a group of men singing, playing drums and flutes, and carrying a brightly painted portable shrine on their shoulders. It was a Sufi *moulid*, a festival for a Sufi saint. I had never before heard such lively, haunting music. We all listened, enraptured, until the procession was out of sight.

"Now you've seen the real Egypt," Salem told me.

"That has to be the most wonderful music in the world," I said.

"And never was piping so sad / And never was piping so gay," Mamoun quoted, and I turned to stare at him in astonishment. Later, I learned that a few years before, two Irish volunteers had taught at Qena, passing on to their students their own love of Yeats, so the apt quotation was not as utterly remarkable as I had supposed. And yet no words could have described more eloquently what we had just heard.

"It's sadder when you understand the words," Salem pointed out. "They're all about how loving God is like loving an unattainable woman."

"If you like Sufi music, maybe we'll make a Saeedia of you yet," Mamoun said heartily, breaking the spell as the car started up again.

I felt flattered, and we moved on.

I was still thinking about this and remembering the music when abruptly, in the middle of Luxor, our taxi slammed on its brakes again. A young woman had stepped off the sidewalk almost in front of the cab. Salem's face was a mask of shock and horror as he and Mamoun began talking to each other in Arabic.

"It's her, it's Aisha," Mamoun explained quickly, as Salem shook my hand and apologized for not being able to see me off at the airport. Out of the rear window, I watched him and a young woman in a headscarf and black trousers slowly disappear in the dust and the crowd, and I wondered if that would be the last time I would ever see him.

"What's going on? What is she doing here?" I wanted to know.

Mamoun looked almost as worried as Salem had, his lips pursed and a deep line rippling across his forehead. "I don't know," he said.

"But it doesn't look good." Then he added, "I'm sorry to involve you in our Saeedi problems like this. You must think us very primitive."

Well, yes, I did, until I reflected that primitive people probably don't apologize for seeming primitive, especially in moments of crisis like this one.

I didn't find out until weeks later what had happened, and it was years before I learned the story's conclusion. Aisha had somehow found out (the note? Mamoun didn't know and Salem wouldn't tell me) that Salem was going to the Luxor airport and she had run away to try to find him, hoping that they could elope to Cairo. Although they would probably be found and killed, she thought that this would be better than marrying someone else. This, at least, was the reasoning of a sheltered twenty-one-year-old woman desperately in love for the first time in her life. Salem wasn't so sure. For the time being, Salem decided, she had to go home.

That evening Mamoun, at some risk to himself, took her back to her family, explaining that she had become upset and gone to stay with one of her female friends in Qena. As her teacher, he thought it appropriate to take her home, in case her absence was misunderstood. "They were polite," he told me, "but they obviously didn't believe me. I told them I would give them my word that Salem would drop any attempt to see her. They didn't believe me about that either. I didn't care. I was just glad they didn't start shooting as soon as they saw us, thinking I must be Salem."

And because they didn't believe him they spend the next several weeks following Salem around. Every time he stepped outside, he would see one of her relatives standing there with folded arms, glaring at him. This was just to let him know that if he had any ideas of trying to meet with Aisha, he should drop them. "He was so afraid that he wouldn't even go out alone to buy food. Someone had to go with him, like a chaperone," Mamoun told me. But later, Aisha's family tried a different ploy. They agreed to the marriage, but asked a dower (the money the groom advances toward the establishment of the new household) far beyond Salem's means. When he didn't pursue the marriage then, Aisha became convinced that he didn't really love her. She had been willing to give her life to marry him, but he, it seemed, was unwilling to go into debt to marry her.

The story has a strange sequel. Five years later, when Salem was in his early thirties, he did make it to the United States, part of an arrangement through his university to do research for his doctoral dissertation at the University of Pittsburgh. Aisha had married one of her *Ashraf* kinsmen two or three years earlier. Mamoun and I were then on our way from Washington to Illinois, but we met Salem in a Denny's near Pittsburgh and spent an afternoon talking about all that had happened.

Salem looked much older. Thin before, he now looked emaciated, with deep lines around his mouth. It was as if the cheerful, good-looking young man I had known in Egypt had shrunken and soured. And he was now flirting with political Islam rather than unattainable young women, in part as a response to the culture shock of living in the United States, in part because of deteriorating political conditions in Egypt. The results, in fact, were surprisingly similar. After publishing letters to the editor opposing the Gulf War and defending Islam in a Pittsburgh newspaper, he had received so many threatening calls and letters that he was again afraid to go out of his house alone. Perhaps America is not as free of tribalism as one might suppose.

But at least he was still alive. A few years after I left, a young woman graduate from Qena who was from a tribal Arab family had married a *fellah* and eloped with him to Cairo. Three months later, her cousin killed them. Salem and Mamoun knew all of them, the girl, her husband, and her cousin. The girl had been the village beauty, who had nevertheless been determined to go to college and become a school teacher. Her husband had been one of her colleagues. The cousin seemed to Mamoun and Salem like an intelligent, gentle young man and was also a college graduate. Now two of them were dead and the other in prison for the rest of his life.

"So I guess I'm lucky," Salem told me.

I didn't know any of this that afternoon in Luxor. I didn't even know if Mamoun would be alive in two weeks time, and I was beginning to fall in love with him.

"Don't worry. It will all work out somehow," he told me as I passed through the metal detector and boarded the plane.

The plane was full of other Westerners, all with sunburns and carrying shopping bags full of carved alabaster sphinxes and hand-worked brass plates with pictures of Cleopatra and Tutankhamen on them. I looked around and knew that I had escaped, escaped back into my own world, like Kirk and Spock, who can just say, "Beam me up" and be back in a familiar, artificial, technological world, away from violence and primal emotions. I moved through other worlds, but could escape only into my own. Salem and Mamoun moved through so many worlds with greater understanding, but could finally escape into mine only at differing costs. And perhaps I had escaped at a cost also, as well as escaping my own tribe without knowing it at the time. As the plane rose above Luxor, I thought of Mamoun going back now into the city to look for Salem and Aisha. I thought of Salem, trying to explain to a desperate and hysterical girl that they could have both their lives and what gave them meaning if they could only wait, when both of them knew that wasn't true. I heard again the Sufi music, and thought of the poetry of love and longing transmuted into a love of God that went with that music, all in words I could not understand; I saw again the desperate gaiety of Salem and Mamoun, both so determined that their crisis should not interfere with my enjoying myself, both so shaped by a culture to which I could only react as I had to that music, enthralled with the sound without knowing the words. When I looked at the blond American woman with sunburned shoulders sitting across the aisle from me, chatting happily with her husband about their purchases, a version of myself, perhaps, just a few months earlier, she seemed stranger to me than anything I had seen in Egypt.

13

Twain on the Nile

The year 1985–86 was when the security police mutinied in Cairo as well as the year when American fighter jets bombed Libya. It was also the one-hundredth anniversary of the publication of *The Adventures of Huckleberry Finn*. I was teaching the novel as part of some additional work I was doing at the College of Arts in Mansoura, and as the months passed, I wondered if I were living it as well.

My students saw some parallels too. Noting that all the most violent episodes took place after Huck and Jim had mistakenly drifted past their original destination of Cairo, Illinois, and observing that Cairo, Egypt, was the traditional boundary between upper and lower Egypt, one young woman claimed to be quite sure of Twain's meaning. "Twain shows us the universal truth," she pointed out, to the great amusement of her classmates "that once you travel south of Cairo, the people are all crazy."

Maybe so. After all, Twain came from north of Cairo, just as she did. I was tempted to play with the idea a little more after reading about the current north/south division of the world that has not only encompassed economics and politics but also values and perceptions. I wondered if this is always the north's view the south, whether it is Mansoura looking at the Saeed or Europe looking at Africa or America looking at Latin America. We just start the south in different places.

I also couldn't help wondering about my own parallels, as I drifted through the political upheavals of that year. I knew that what had happened with Aisha and Salem was not an Egyptian version of the Shephardson-Grangerford feud. It proved, after all, to be a bloodless tragedy, unlike the violence about which Twain wrote. I'm sure everyone who has read the novel remembers the episode, with two families of Mississippi planters locked in a blood feud whose cause neither knows anymore. When young Sophia Grangerford elopes with Harney

Shephardson, almost all the Grangerford men die in the ensuing bloodbath, not only armed men but children like Huck's alter ego, Buck Grangerford, and wounded and unarmed people fleeing for their lives, all in the name of preserving honor. Twain's sympathies seem to be with the two young people, who are trying to replace the meaningless bloodshed with a union; I have always seen it as a parallel to the Civil War, and perhaps to war in general. Yet finally the feud, in its ferocity and indiscriminateness, always seemed to me a very American kind of violence. So perhaps I was wrong in feeling that I was living Twain that year in Egypt. Even the time I was nearer to actual violence, when I was standing on the balcony of the Fulbright flat in Zamalek listening to the gunfire a half-mile away, across the river in Giza, I wondered that.

During the police mutiny I had felt like I was Huck, caught up in a feud I didn't understand. I was under a curfew. From my window, I could see armored personnel carriers and, later, tanks rolling through the city streets. Although I never saw a single casualty myself, hundreds of people were killed not more than a mile from where I whiled away my time rereading Twain and making notes for the rest of the semester's lectures. And yet it was all a curiously Egyptian type of crisis.

I had come to Cairo to see another Fulbright teacher off at the airport along with one of our students, a droll, lanky boy named Bassam who always wore jeans and seemed a great deal like an American kid his age, except that he had been brought up to be more polite to his elders (me, for example) than most of his American counterparts. He knew the driver and had arranged the trip, so it seemed only fair that he should come along; the trip to Cairo was something of an adventure for him and also, he thought, it would give him a chance to see his girlfriend, who had moved to Cairo with her parents a few months earlier. We intended to drive from Mansoura, spend one night in Cairo before seeing the man off at the airport the next morning, and return to Mansoura late in the afternoon.

Such was the plan. But in the morning, the taxi driver we had hired in Mansoura showed up with a cheerful-looking middle-aged army officer sitting beside him. "There was some trouble last night," the driver, who I think was one of Bassam's relatives, explained, as Bassam translated. "So I thought I should bring Aziz with me in case there are roadblocks on the way to the airport." Aziz was on leave, but he was wearing his uniform to deter anyone who might try to stop us.

Aziz stepped out of the car, shook hands with all of us, and then told the whole story to Bassam, who in turn, explained it to us as we tried to make our way to the airport.

The night before, some of the security police had revolted, attacking nightclubs out toward the pyramids and reportedly setting fires around the airport. Yet at first nothing looked out of the ordinary that clear February morning. The sun was shining, people were on their way to work, and Aziz did not seem terribly concerned. He stroked his graying moustache as he explained it to us.

In fact, he was quite sympathetic with the rebels, who, he said, were conscripted into the security force, paid next to nothing, forced to live in the most unsanitary conditions (it later came out that epidemics of cholera had swept the security police barracks), and then put to work standing in the sun all day guarding the big nightclubs, tourist hotels, and embassies, where everyone they saw spent more for lunch than they made in a year. Most of them, he said, were illiterate Saeedis, illiterate because their parents had to take them out of school to work in the fields or face starvation. Apparently, Egypt was a much poorer country than seeing the rich farmland of the Nile delta had lead me to believe. "You can't treat any human being that way," he said to us in English.

We came to the first army roadblock on a wide tree-lined boulevard in Heliopolis and were waved through when the soldier saw Aziz. True, the soldier was armed, but it looked like the sort of rifle color guards carry in parades, not something that anyone was going to be shot with. Past the roadblock, we saw fewer and fewer cars, suggesting to me that something might indeed be happening. Yet the driver and Aziz and Bassam were all cheerfully smoking one another's cigarettes (they offered packs of cigarettes in rounds, like Brits do with drinks) and making jokes as if we were all just out for a morning's drive. Tonight, I told myself, the teacher will be on his way back to the States, I will be back in Mansoura, and I won't have to think any more about this until I'm ready.

At the second roadblock we were turned back. The airport was closed. The driver turned on the radio and the jokes and the English temporarily stopped.

"What's going on?"

"Nobody knows yet, exactly," Bassam told me.

When we reached the first roadblock again, an armored personnel carrier rolled past us.

"What do you call that in English?" Bassam wanted to know.

I told him that it was either a tank or an armored personnel carrier, I wasn't sure, but I thought that if it were a tank, it would have a big gun sticking out of the front of it.

"One good thing about this," he pointed out. "I'm learning many new English words and phrases. 'Roadblock,' 'armored personnel carrier,' 'tank.' But what happened to 'metaphor,' 'foil character,' and 'personification'?"

The traffic suddenly became thicker. Cairo is normally a continual traffic jam, but this was different. Instead of the usual cheerful and varied throng, the sidewalks were filled with worried-looking people. And although jaywalkers normally wound their ways through six lanes of shifting traffic unscathed and unconcerned, I saw the bumper of a Fiat hit the leg of an old man in a *gellabeyeh*. More startling still, no crowd gathered to berate the driver. The old man just looked at his bruised leg, shouted at the driver, and hurried on. Finally, the traffic stopped entirely.

"There's a curfew," Bassam explained to me. "Everybody is supposed to be in their houses by two."

I looked at my watch. It was now one thirty and we obviously weren't going anywhere. The crowd on foot, however, seemed to have thinned out. It was the people in the cars that were stuck. One by one, they started getting out of their cars and striking up conversations with one another. The main topic of discussion was whether a coup was going on, and Aziz's opinion seemed much in demand. "Not yet," he told people, who shrugged and got back in their cars.

We were now in Garden City, across the Nile from the flat in Zamalek and from Agouza, where Aziz lived. All bridges, he reported to us, were blocked. But the curfew had just been extended until four o'clock, as all of middle-class Cairo (the car owners) was now stuck in traffic because of the closed bridges. The army was moving some heavy equipment, he told us. What kind of "heavy equipment," I wondered, and thought again of the armored personnel carriers. Surely, in Egypt's midday heat, they would be moving soldiers in trucks unless there was a very good chance they would be shot at.

And yet people now looked far less troubled. From nowhere, kids with bags of sandwiches and canned soda hawked their wares among the stopped and stalled cars at only half again the normal price. I suppose they knew that if they were too greedy, the drivers would leave their cars and walk to the lunch stands themselves.

"There's some moral in this about the triumph of capitalism," I observed. It all seemed very Egyptian to me, that when a political crisis was brewing, people would be buying sandwiches and making jokes.

I thought of this again, two days later, when the airport reopened but was admitting only ticketed passengers into the building and soldiers with mean-looking rifles and fixed bayonets guarded the entrance. Because no one could tell whether the planes would actually take off, Bassam and Aziz and I sat in the car, along with a graduate student from Cairo who had come to say goodbye to his teacher. He assured us he hadn't heard of any crisis, although he was a member of the army reserve. I wondered if he were the only person in Cairo who didn't know.

Meanwhile Bassam and I, bored with waiting and curious to see what was actually going on in the airport, discovered that we could enter the airport through the baggage area. A couple of soldiers, busy drinking tea and playing cards, made no move to stop us, and thus to our amazement, we found ourselves in the international departure lounge, along with the departing teacher who had gone through a half-dozen security checks to get where he was. He stared at us.

"How did you get here?" He wanted to know.

"Genies," Bassam told him.

And yet at the same time that these comedies were going on, a very real tragedy was taking place in the streets. For two days, we had been listening to gunfire from across the Nile, and I could reasonably assume, I felt, that some of those shots were hitting people. My companions in the Fulbright flat were less concerned. The two American graduate students had left, and in their place was a Syrian woman who was married to another of the Fulbright teachers. She was blasé about the whole thing.

"I've lived through two wars and ten attempted coups," she pointed out. "Now I don't care about things like this as long as nobody is shooting at me."

And of course, nobody was shooting at us. If Huck watched the worst of the battle between the Shepardsons and the Grangerfords from a tree, I had a far higher and safer vantage point from the top-floor apartment in Zamalek. I had no idea what the fighting was really about, and neither, apparently, did many of the participants. I wondered how many in the army, like Aziz, sympathized with the rebellious security forces.

Nor was it entirely clear why the forces had mutinied and why they had chosen that particular time. Why were they attacking tourist hotels and nightclubs rather than government buildings? Why, indeed, had they chosen a violent mutiny when a mass strike would have brought their cause widespread public support? Who was the real target, and how did the security policemen, armed only with rifles and pistols, think they were going to defeat the Egyptian army's tanks? According to what I read later, hundreds of the security police were killed and thousands arrested, with no casualties on the side of the army. And some of those arrested were carrying large amounts of money, causing the Mubarak regime to assert (without any subsequent evidence) that they had been paid to revolt by Libyan agents. My graduate students were all very skeptical of this claim, pointing out that Egypt's internal problems were always the fault of whatever regime America did not like at the time. They offered the alternative explanation that the revolt had been sponsored by drug lords to force the resignation of Ahmed Rushdie, the minister of Interior, who had been cracking down on drugs and organized crime. If that was true, it worked. But no one knew for sure, even the men doing the fighting, and no clear explanation ever emerged. It remained as bloody and meaningless as the feud.

Instead of answers, I heard rumors and continued to hear rumors for months to come. The most disturbing one to me at the time was that the security forces had attacked the Israeli embassy, killing several Israeli diplomats; the Israelis were going to bomb Cairo in retaliation, the story went. It sounded like a wild story to me, the sort of thing that the expats in Saudi Arabia would have made up to terrify one another. Nevertheless, it made me nervous. When I went out to the roof to collect my laundry from the clothesline, I couldn't help feeling that I was in a different Cairo. In the streets below, the crowds of pedestrians, the taxis, and the mobs of cars were replaced by a solitary jeep or truck cruising the empty canyons of the city and instead of the noise of the traffic came the sound of distant gunfire. How far did the sound travel? I wondered. I scanned the sky for Israeli planes and thought about how unfair it was that I could be killed because of the actions of people I could not begin to understand, In fact, I got as far as wondering if my death would be mentioned on the American newscasts, and I was working myself into a rage at the idea that it might be covered up, before the sound of artillery from across the Nile reminded me of the fact that I, after all, was not the one who was in immediate danger. My only problems were a diet of canned goods and the company of people with whom I would not have chosen to be marooned on a desert island. Perhaps I was more like the ever-fanciful Tom Sawyer than Huck.

And yet perhaps my fears were not as far-fetched as I had convinced myself at the time. A week later, driving past the Israeli embassy in Dokki, I noted it was still surrounded by tanks, their guns pointed outward at the now-peaceful residential streets. Dokki was on the same side of the Nile as the worst areas of the fighting. And after all, the Reagan and the Clinton administrations would later bomb civilians in Arab capitals with far less provocation than the current rumor had given the Israelis.

In fact, it was only a short time later that U.S. planes bombed Tripoli and Benghazi, killing dozens of people not so different from my students and their families. For weeks, the students had been pestering me at the beginning of every class, wanting to know what I thought was going to happen between the United States and Libya.

"Nothing," I would tell them. "It's all just a lot of political hot air. Now will you please turn to today's assignment."

Then one morning, while I was listening to the BBC World Service on my shortwave radio, I heard Reagan explaining why it had been necessary to bomb Libya that night.

One of my graduate students, Reda, a polite, earnest young man who was a full-time junior high school teacher in a village twenty-five miles away, had invited me to stop at his home to meet his family and his students before I continued on to Cairo and the AUC library. I wondered, as I waited for him downstairs in the lobby of my apartment building, if he would still show up. It was hard to imagine life just continuing normally. But he arrived, although he was looking unusually grave.

"Have you heard the news?" I asked him as we got into the taxi together.

"I think everyone has heard the news," Reda told me. We rode for a few moments in silence. "There's an Arabic fable," he said finally, "about the rat and the lion. The rat keeps biting the lion's tale when he is sleeping, and the other animals all say to him, 'Why don't you kill the rat?' and the lion answers, 'Because it would be too easy, and it would bring me no glory.' Now the lion has killed the rat. But he can't pretend that it has brought him glory."

I said nothing. And realizing that I might not feel comfortable discussing it, Reda didn't bring it up again, and neither did any of his friends or students who crowded round me to ask questions when we got to the village. Instead, they asked me about farming methods in the United States (they were politely skeptical of my assertion that where I came from, farmers didn't need to irrigate their crops), and how American literature was different from British literature (I suspected Reda of having primed them to ask that one), and if their way of living seemed primitive to me.

And they were poor. Water came from a hand pump in the courtyard, and the floor of the reception room where the family entertained me was beaten earth. But it actually wasn't much different from some of the farms in rural western Pennsylvania I had visited when I was growing up in the late fifties and early sixties; some of my friends back then had shallow wells that went dry every summer, chemical toilets, and woodstoves in the kitchen that were the main source of heat all winter. The big difference was their courtesy to strangers. Here, the young men and women of the village, mostly people who had finished high school and could speak some English, came in to meet me and ask questions. Children filed in one by one to shake hands with me, greet me, stare at me with their thickly lashed big brown eyes, and then leave after a few moments. I found this phenomenon curious until I saw Reda's mother standing in the doorway admitting the children one by one.

"They all want to have a look at me, and she's telling them that if they want to see me, they can come in and shake hands with me and introduce themselves instead of standing outside staring at me like I was an animal in a zoo," I suggested.

Reda was astonished. "How did you know that? That's exactly what she said. But she said it in Arabic. How did you understand?"

I was tempted to leave him with the impression that I really understood Arabic much better than he had supposed.

When I left to catch the bus for Cairo a couple of hours later, some of the young married women of the village were waiting for me.

"These ladies are a little superstitious," Reda told me. "They think that if they look at you, their babies will grow up to be as pretty as you are." Apparently, my height and light skin were the desired attributes. Flattered but embarrassed, I managed to say that if their babies grew up to be as pretty as they were, they would be lucky indeed. And this was true. These fresh-faced young women, with their naturally red cheeks and sparkling eyes, were prettier than the town girls with all their make-up and their careful adherence to decorous behavior. These women just smiled at the compliment, which I think they took for mere politeness. Normally, I feel very awkward when I meet people for the first time, but Reda and his family refused to let me feel that way. I shook so many hands and kissed so many babies I began to feel as if I were running for governor. When I mentioned this to Reda, he laughed and told me he thought I could win in his district.

In fact, I had such a good time that I forgot all about the bombing of Libya until I arrived in Cairo, where one of the American teachers was denouncing it as terrorism and demanding to know if I agreed.

"I don't know what to think," I told him honestly. "I suppose what concerns me right now is whether or not this makes it more likely that somebody is going to blow up my plane when I leave here."

This was self-interested enough to make him stop trying to argue politics with me. I recalled this conversation years later when I heard about the Pan Am jet that exploded over Scotland and thought that one of those passengers could have been me. I also remembered that night in Cairo when we thought the Israelis would bomb the city, and I thought some of those people under the bombs in Tripoli could have been like me, too. But more probably, most of them would have been like those Egyptians villagers who had welcomed me to their homes the day of the bombing.

It would be a long time before I could sort through all my feelings. This was not like the police mutiny, which had nothing to do with me. In this, I felt implicated, if only because of my nationality, and this made it all the more difficult to know how to judge what had happened. If the police mutiny had confused many of the English-speaking Egyptians I knew, their condemnations of the bombings were unequivocal, putting me on the defensive. The security police, however illiterate, abused, and misguided, had arms and were fighting back. The people killed in the air raid were unarmed men, women, and children, Egyptians pointed out to me. One student even left a graphic picture on my desk of the charred and mangled bodies of some of the child victims. Accompanying it was a note that read, "Does this make you proud of your country?" Actually, I thought this was a rather mean-spirited reaction, and the student did have the decency to apologize later. Yet these pictures were apparently widely circulated in the Arab world; I wondered if any of the American newspapers had carried them, and what the response had been if they had.

I wanted to believe that the bombing might have had some larger, justifying purpose. Certainly, in his radio address, Reagan had been at his most convincing, so much so that even though I opposed most of his policies, I wondered if he might have been right this time. At the time, it just seemed too easy to blame the evil Americans, and when anyone asked me what I thought, I could only answer, "I don't know. I don't know."

It wasn't until some weeks later, when I began to read the accounts in American magazines and newspapers, that my emotions began to find a center. I was shocked by the reporters' and commentators' total lack of moral questioning, indeed, by their assumption that the raid had not been merely justifiable, but brave and noble. The gloating pointed to something ugly in the American character, something that had been around for a long time but that only a few people like Twain had dared to depict and indict.

I thought of the episode in *Huckleberry Finn*, which I had just finished teaching a few weeks before, in which Colonel Sherburn kills the harmless town drunk, Boggs. Boggs is on one of his biannual rips, riding around town yelling insults and threats at Colonel Sherburn. Everyone knows that Boggs will never follow through on these threats and is amused by it all until Sherburn feels that his honor cannot tolerate the insults any more, gives Boggs a deadline to get out of town, and then, when Boggs ignores the deadline, shoots him down in the street, leaving him to die in the arms of his sixteen-year-old daughter.

Protecting honor had once meant a duel between armed equals in which both men fired into the air or at least had the option of doing so, not the killing of an unarmed man who is begging for his life. Twain shows that Sherburn's act is wanton cruelty and abuse of power disguised as defending honor. And yet the disguise works; Sherburn's concept of honor prevails. How different from that is the idea that the world's major military and political power can restore its national honor by killing the unprotected citizens of a small third-world country.

Of course, the parallel is not exact. Libyan agents may or may not have been involved in the bombing of the Berlin nightclub that was the declared provocation for the air raid. In fact, I recall reading later that the agents were from Syria, not Libya, and indeed that Libya had not been involved at all. If the motive was revenge, it was certainly indiscriminate and disproportionate, and if it was to deter terrorism, it obviously did not work—at least if Libyans were behind the bombing of the Pan Am jet over Scotland. I kept hoping to read of some better reason and coming up with nothing.

And so I was left with Boggs and Sherburn. One of my graduate students suggested that it was as if Sherburn had killed not Boggs, but his daughter. All my students were making bitter jokes about how many American bombers it took to kill one Libyan baby, and they also pointed out that when IRA bombs went off in London, British jets did not bomb Catholic sections of Northern Ireland. Given the level of official tension between Egypt and Libya at that time, I often wondered if the vehemence of their responses came not from an ethical or political stance, exactly, but from the sense that they could just as easily have been the victims themselves, with the same triumphant reaction from the mainstream American press and public. Or perhaps these were not their thoughts. After all, most of them could not afford to buy American newspapers. But they were certainly my thoughts as the year continued. I began to wonder why I was teaching American literature to Arab students, trying to show them the America of Twain and Thoreau, an America that was morally aware and self-critical, when none of this seemed to show in America's dealings with Arabs. Maybe they were better off with the stereotypes they had derived from *Dallas* and B movies, I sometimes thought.

Nevertheless, as far as I could see, my students didn't seem harmed by my efforts. They seemed to find Twain funny and thought-provoking and to be happier to read him than the usual English-major fare of Shakespeare, Pope, and Defoe. I was the one who loved Twain and was now in danger of turning into a crank because of the disparity between what I had seen and what I believed in.

Lines and images and ideas from Twain echoed in my mind during my next three years in the Middle East and after. In my most bitter moments, I felt that my Mansoura student's joke that everybody south of Cairo was crazy seemed to have become a geopolitical guideline in the industrialized north's view of the underdeveloped south; the lives of everyone south of the Caribbean or Mediterranean had become expendable. And when American generals spoke of the low number of casualties in the Gulf War, although it cost the lives of thousands of Third World "guest workers" and hundreds of thousands of Iraqis, I thought of what happened when Huck told Aunt Sally that he was delayed because of an explosion on his steamboat. She says,

"Good gracious! Anybody hurt?"

"No'm. Killed a nigger."

"Well, it's lucky, because sometimes people do get hurt."

14

ꙮ

Misreadings

If literature is a bridge between cultures, then it is a narrow hanging bridge with missing slats that only a few rare people dare try to cross. And even they often need some help. Everyone else devotes most of his energies to convincing himself that the bridge is not worth crossing anyway.

Teaching in Egypt was the first time I had encountered so many foreign students trying to grapple with the literature of another culture. Of course, I had taught fiction to Arab students before, in Saudi Arabia, but there, classes were small enough for my students and me to get to know each other and to develop a rapport. Many of the students were fairly well trained in interpreting literature, and the rest had the notes handed down from older sisters to give them at least a sense of the standard interpretations of the works. For them, literature was an intellectual exercise of exploring patterns, themes, and ideas for the good students, and of remembering the main points of the lectures for the average ones. Thanks to Egypt's lack of libraries and the fact that no one had taught these particular works at the college before, my Egyptian students had to rely on their own reactions. For this, they incorporated what they thought they knew of American society, based on American TV and movies, and what they thought they knew of universal human nature, based on twenty years of living in a provincial city in the Nile delta. In short, they responded with the same honest naïveté with which most American undergraduates react to the literature of another time, another place, another culture—anything other than contemporary American fiction. Only the assumptions themselves differed.

My Egyptian students seemed to respond to nineteenth-century American literature rather like the culture-shocked Americans I had known had reacted to Saudi Arabia. Lost in another culture, they looked for anything that looked or sounded familiar to act as a guide-post. They assumed that when events seemed similar to ones in their culture, these events had precisely the same causes. They looked for what confirmed their stereotypes about Western culture, not necessarily out of malice, but because it was something familiar. Looking for similarities, they saw the Shepherdson-Grangerford feud as exactly the same as a Saeedi blood feud. Such feuds had disappeared from the Nile delta generations ago, but my students still understood the motivations behind them very well. They knew that if these disputes were not about property, then they were about the sexual honor of women. Thus, some students refused to believe that the Grangerfords did not really know the origin of the feud; the adults, they reasoned, just did not want to explain it to Huck or to Buck Grangerford because it involved sexual honor, and the boys were too young to hear about such things. The same students assumed that when Harney eloped with Sophia, he had no intention of actually marrying her, but planned to revenge himself on the Grangerfords by ruining her reputation. One young man, in fact, declared that I was "too kindly and innocent" in my thinking if I believed that Harney would actually marry Sophia.

These students seemed to be reading a different book than I was. And if there was not any support for what they thought in the text itself, there were few explicit statements to contradict it, which made their response all the more reasonable and difficult to refute. To prove the standard interpretation of the work, I had only Twain's sympathetic tone toward Sophia and Harney, and Twain's repeated insistence on the cruelty and irrationality of mobs, of whom the Shepardsons and Grangerfords were but another variation; that, and all that came from knowing the history and culture of the society for which it was written and in which it took place, and from knowing the traditions of Western literature. I read them the concluding speech from *Romeo and Juliet,* and explained that Twain was assuming that his readers would know the play and draw the same inferences from his story. Only a dozen or so students could see this. But perhaps that even that many did was more remarkable than I first thought.

They also had problems with the character of Lily Bart, the virginal but slandered heroine of Edith Wharton's *House of Mirth.* The plotline seems at first like that of a standard nineteenth-century novel. Orphaned and without money of her own, Lily is taken in by a wealthy aunt who is willing to subsidize Lily's search through turn-of-the-century New York's upper class for a wealthy and socially acceptable husband. The problem is that Lily is too fussy; she wants a man who is interesting and intelligent as well as rich, and thus cannot really throw herself into the chase. When she continues unmarried, rumors spread that she is having affairs, her former friends begin to shun her, and she ends up disinherited and destitute. For balance, and to show that Lily's own indecisiveness and impulsiveness are as responsible for what happens to her as is the shallowness of her society, Wharton contrasts Lily with her plain friend Gertie, who lives alone on her meager income and survives on the margins of the society in which Lily at first seems to thrive. The novel is a complex analysis of the position of women in early twentieth-century America and of a society dominated both by wealth and by the appearance of propriety.

I thought that this story had certain parallels to contemporary Egypt—the closely knit society, the emphasis on premarital virginity, the tendency to judge by appearances and to gossip. But many of my students not only failed to see any resemblance, they thought they were reading a novel version of *Dallas*. A few thought that of course Lily was having affairs. That's what Western women did. She was just pretending to be virtuous to trap unsuspecting men, because, of course, any man would want to marry a virgin rather than a slut. Poor wilted Lily. But more blamed her undeserved decline in society on neither the greed and superficiality of the people around her or on her own limited insights, but on the fact that she was not chaperoned and protected by the men in her family. She was given too much freedom and not enough protection and support. In short, it was what was different in American society that was the cause of Lily's problems, not any of the things that American and Egyptian society had in common.

Sometimes these ideas came out in class discussions, but with over a hundred students in a class, the misconceptions were hard to explain and correct. More frequently, the students would voice these ideas after class, when a dozen or so were clustered around me to ask questions. I had mixed feelings about these sessions. They wanted to argue with me; they needed to be right; they were bright enough to see that what I was saying and what they were reading called their whole sense of the world into question; they were taking literature seriously, at least as a threat to complacency. So even though I was tired after a long day of teaching, I would sit in the courtyard on one of the dilapidated benches while they elbowed each other out of the way, hissed down students who phrased their questions too rudely, and shushed each other while I tried to explain once again the distinction between selfishness and individualism and why Twain hated mobs. Every once in a while, I would turn the tables and ask them if Wharton's upper-crust society was just another version of a Twain mob, or what criticisms they thought Twain or Wharton might make of Egyptian society. Every one of them seemed to have an answer, thought out or not, that demanded immediate airing. It was fun, but I sometimes wondered how much it had to do with social assertion and how much it had to do with learning.

Later some of the women, tired of being pushed to the peripheries of these after-class discussions, would visit me in my apartment. Here we had time for more leisurely talks. We drank tea and nibbled cookies and discussed at length why Lily Bart's aunt disowned her, before we went on to the ways in which both Arab and American society commodified women. In these little groups of three or four I began to feel that a real intellectual exchange was taking place. Whether or not they learned from it, I certainly did.

Thinking over their reactions, I began to wonder if the problem was more complex than the search for the familiar, but was in fact part of the far larger problem of distinguishing between what in literature is universal, what is unique to a particular time and place, and how to judge those things that are unique to a time and place other than one's own. The easiest and most comfortable thing to do was to decide that what was wrong with the society they read about was unique to it (for example, Lily Bart had too much freedom), while ignoring differences between the societies that would suggest the variety of human experience and motivations. Some students stopped with this answer. Others admitted their confusion and started groping for the more difficult answers, beginning with discarding the assumptions that their own society was superior to the one the writer was criticizing, that they could know all about another society without ever having lived in it, that any society is static or monolithic, and the final and most difficult assumption, that they not only knew all about "those people" but about human nature itself. These may be the hardest things that any reader can do.

Most of these students had to ask a great many questions, however, before they could come to such an understanding. Why, several girls wanted to know, did a beautiful young woman like Lily Bart go around unchaperoned by anyone in her family if a woman's reputation for chastity was so vitally important back then? Didn't anyone realize that envious people would make things up, no matter how Lily behaved? And why didn't her family introduce her to suitable men, rather than leaving it up to her to find someone? Wasn't this negligence bordering on cruelty, to make a girl find her own way in society and then blame her if she made the wrong choices? It was hard to find an adequate answer. Lily was not the sort of pliant ingenue to marry whomever others deemed suitable. How could I explain that this was at least a limited sort of freedom, not just indifference or negligence on the part of her family? And I tried to explain the difference between American puritanism, which tried to suppress sexuality by pretending that it didn't exist, and their kind of Mediterranean puritanism, which was ever alert to the dangers of sexuality, real or imaginary. Having been raised in an era when girls were allowed to make out for hours in the back seats of cars but were expected to be virgins when they married, I thought I could understand the psychology behind the attitudes of Lily's society. Yet how could I explain it to students who thought it was reasonable, if a little strict, for a twenty-two-year-old woman to come to her woman teacher's apartment chaperoned by her ten-year-old brother?

They had other questions as well. If Western society was so much more progressive than Arab society, why hadn't an upper-class woman like Lily gone to college? Why could she find only menial jobs after she had been disinherited? My students could not imagine any reason that a family would not educate a girl unless they objected to her mixing with men, which was obviously not the case with Lily. I did my best to explain the evolution of women's rights in America, at the same time realizing how simplistic had been my own assumption that turn-of-the-century New York was very like modern-day Cairo. In fact, my assumption may have been similar to that of my students who decided that the Shephersons and the Grangerfords were engaged in a Saeedi blood feud.

Educated Egyptian men, these students pointed out to me, wanted to marry educated women. In fact, it was becoming a problem in the villages, where the bright boys would go to university but the girls they would ordinarily have married were kept home because their parents didn't want them traveling to the school in taxis or worse, staying in the dormitories. The result was that these girls of unquestionable virtue remained unmarried while their young men married town girls they had met in college. Why didn't the men of Lily Bart's time insist on educated women? they wanted to know. I told them the answer to that was in a novel called *The Bostonians*, and tried to summarize it. Educated women were often ridiculed and viewed as unfeminine, even by educated men; education was thought to be unnatural in women. There were few jobs for women, and even professional women faced mistrust and discrimination. My students were shocked. Women not as smart as men? Brains and femininity didn't go together? What a silly idea!

I'm not sure I would conclude from this that Arab society has traditionally seen women as tempting rather than inferior, as some of the women I talked to claimed. And perhaps having a university degree simply made an Egyptian woman more of a trophy. Perhaps the wit of Arab women in traditional Arabic literature, which my students were so eager to tell me about, reveals no more about the actual status of Arab women that the cleverness of Shakespeare's heroines does about Elizabethan women. But certainly, the sexism of the Arab world is not the same creature as the sexism of the West. Beware the glib analogy, I told myself.

As a result of these talks, rambling and defensive as they sometimes became, my best students began to understand the novel in its own context and to see its relevance to their own understanding of the world. They began by realizing that the turn-of-the-century New York of Edith Wharton was not *Dallas* and that they did not know the social customs of Lily Bart and her circle. American society had changed, just as theirs had. And yes, they could see how a young woman like Lily's friend Gertie could live on her own, still be virtuous, and even be fairly happy, and they could see that Gertie was in the novel to show that Lily's problems were the result of her own difficulties in making choices as much as they were of her society. It strained their concept of what was likely to befall a young woman not under the protection of her family and of what they thought was a basic human need for constant companionship, but they were willing to concede that it might be so, and that independence and relative solitude might have their own pleasures for some people. One thoughtful young woman even said she envied not only Gertie's life, but even Lily Bart's freedom to make her own mistakes. "It's better than having to live with someone else's mistaken idea of what's best for you," she said. The women who were with her that day agreed. And I found out later that she spoke from experience. She had been accepted at the American University in Cairo, which had a far better English program, but her parents worried about her reputation and consequent marriageability if she lived in Cairo, even though she would be staying with relatives there. And so she stayed with her parents and attended Mansoura University.

I don't want to imply that anyone's values or ideas changed radically as a result of what we read and discussed. Yet what we had all been exposed to, and what we had all inwardly resisted despite our curiosity, was the existence of another valid way of seeing the world. Of course, this applied only to a dozen or so of the students. The rest, the students who never spoke in class or took part in the after-class sessions, most probably simply took notes, repeated them on the exam, and never gave a thought to the novels again. Even a portion of the after-class arguers remained convinced that the novels revealed the superiority of their own society—although I don't think that they would have argued so vehemently if the novels had not implanted in them the troubling suspicion that societies and people, morality and immorality, were perhaps more complex than they had originally supposed. Later, I hoped, when they were older and less unsure of their own futures, they might be able to reconsider some of what they had read.

Or perhaps they never would. Perhaps being older and more educated might only make them more certain that what they knew of the world was the only possibly truth. I thought this some years later, when I read the Western reviews of the translation of Naguib Mahfouz's Nobel Prize-winning *Cairo Trilogy*. Curiously, Western reviewers in both *TLS* and the *New York Times Book Review* read Mahfouz's *Palace Walk*, the first novel of the *Cairo Trilogy*, in much the same way that my most anti-American students had viewed *The House of Mirth* and *Huckleberry Finn*.

Palace Walk tells the story of a lower-middle-class Cairo family in the 1920s, when Egypt was struggling against colonial rule. The protagonist, Ahmed Abd al-Jawad, however, is more concerned with the tensions in his life that arise from his contradictory impulses toward outward propriety, particularly in respect to the reputations of his wife and children, and his need to gratify his appetites and his ego by drinking with his friends and having affairs with women entertainers. He is strict with his family, even by the standards of his time and place, as the responses of his neighbors make clear. He does not allow the women of his family out of his house, and when his wife, Ameena, disobeys him, he sends her home to her mother for several months. Yet Mahfouz makes it clear that Abd al-Jawad is not a cruel man; utterly self-centered and unreflecting, certainly, but never deliberately malicious. Ameena's punishment is only a punishment to her because she loves him. His confinement of his daughters is neither abusive or terribly unusual in his society, and the daughters bear no psychological scars from it. He is the equivalent of an American father of his time who will not let his daughters wear make-up or go to dances. And although he rails and shouts, he never actually strikes anyone. He is an amazing creation, a complex, emotional, and yet terribly limited man, portrayed with honesty and compassion.

But to read the reviews,* one would think that no Western man had ever had an affair, or bullied his wife, or set up one standard of behavior for his daughters and another for his mistresses. To both, Ahmed Abd al-Jawad was the embodiment of Arab misogyny, cruelty, and oppression of women. Just as my students had at first thought Lily Bart's aunt was cruel not to arrange a marriage for her, applying the customs of their own society to the one they were reading about, the reviewers found Abd al-Jawad monstrous in confining his wife and daughters to the house. One writer compared Abd al-Jawad's double life of bullying his family by day and reveling by night to that of a Nazi prison guard who tortures people during the day and then comes home to play the benevolent family man in the evening. This struck me as hardly a fair judgement of a man who commits no act of violence anywhere in the trilogy, who is himself the victim of the British policy of forcing natives to do unpaid manual labor, and whose beloved son is shot dead by British soldiers while taking part in a legal, peaceful demonstration against colonial rule. Somehow, in the mind of the reviewer, the victim of British racism had become the equivalent of a Nazi. And of course labeling someone a Nazi ends all further explanation and discussion.

With equal perversity, the *New York Times* writer implied that Islam itself condoned Abd al-Jawad's behavior, and that Abd al-Jawad was depraved *because* he was pious. To do this, the writer had to ignore Mahfouz's obvious irony in using the phrase "a pious and depraved life" as well as the fact that early in the novel, the old sheikh whom Mahfouz uses to represent traditional Islam upbraids Abd al-Jawad for his drinking and womanizing. Abd al-Jawad is taken aback, but quickly relieves his misgivings by telling himself that God is forgiving, and continues as before. Mahfouz is analyzing the ways in which

---

* "The Decline of the Grocer," *Times Literary Supplement,* Apr. 27, 1990; "A Pious and Depraved Life," *New York Times Book Review,* Feb. 4, 1990.

people who consider themselves religious can compartmentalize socially inconvenient aspects of their religion, the way people can dissociate religious teachings from actual life. It reminded me of the Shepherdsons and Grangerfords leaving their guns outside the church while listening to a sermon on brotherly love and then shooting at each other on the way home. The only difference is that Abd al-Jawad's transgressions are not violent. And of course, although Mahfouz himself applies the term "depraved" to Abd al-Jawad's failings, drinking with a small circle of friends and having four love affairs in twenty years hardly count as depravity if one compares Abd al-Jawad with most twentieth-century Western fictional protagonists. The reviewer missed all of this in his haste to identify Islam as the cause of Ahmed Abd al-Jawad's personal failings, I suppose because of the natural tendency to see what is different as the cause of what is wrong. To him, Islam allowed Abd al-Jawad to be both pious and depraved. (And Lily Bart would have been all right if her male cousins had kept better control of her.)

It strikes me as sad that even sophisticated readers fail to notice textual evidence that contradicts their stereotypes and sadder still that they are unable to learn from the great masterpieces of other cultures. I suppose, again, it comes from the inability to admit one does not fully understand what is going on and ask those who might know. And the suspicion that one might not understand is further complicated by the fact that the only people who might know are the very people one has stereotyped. How can a respectable person learn anything about himself or the world from a vulgar American slut (Lily Bart, Edith Wharton, me) or a stupid, violent Arab (Ahmed Abd al-Jawad, Naguib Mahfouz, any professor of Arabic literature)?

Of course, not all the Western reviewers responded this way, any more than all the students did. The sympathetic reviewers, however, were generally people who knew Arabic and had lived in Egypt, people whose direct experience had already taught them the falseness of the stereotypes. (Why editors do not routinely assign Arabic literature to such reviewers rather than to reviewers hostile to Arab culture is another question. Might the editors have political motives?) It made me wonder about the extent to which educated adults can modify and enlarge their views of the world through anything other than direct experience, or if, after a certain age, reading literature no longer functions as a way of seeking knowledge. I can hardly hold myself up as a counterexample of broadmindedness, because I never even thought to read Arabic fiction until after I had lived in the Arab world. I don't think this question has any ready answer.

What interests me more is that some of my students were able to surmount the obstacles of culture and prejudice when the hostile reviewers, far more experienced readers and certainly far more accomplished writers, could not. And later, I found that many of my American students were as responsive to pieces of Arabic literature as the best of my Egyptian students had been to American literature. Perhaps it was because they carried less baggage across that narrow hanging bridge and were still agile enough to think in new ways. But finally, I think, it was because these students were both brighter and braver than the critics, something the critics' media access and renown could never alter.

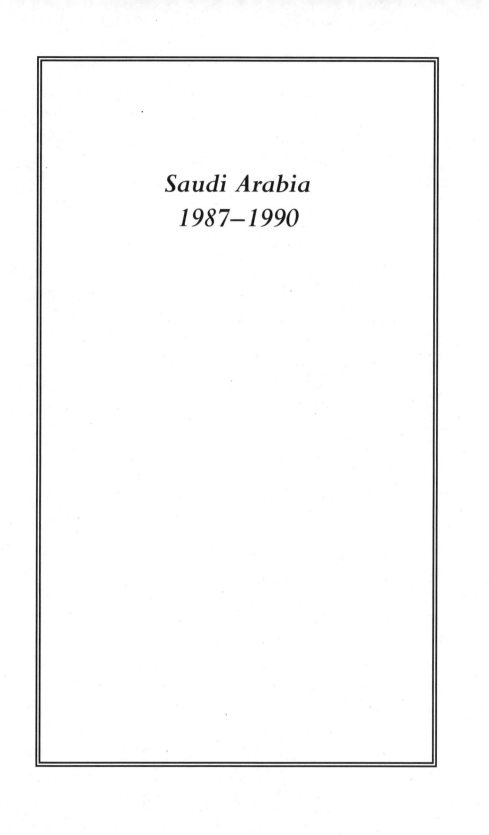

Saudi Arabia
1987–1990

15

Changes

A year and a half after I left Egypt, I was back in Saudi Arabia, where I spent the next two and a half years. I came back to a Saudi Arabia superficially changed, but one into which I could now see a little more deeply.

My own life had changed as well, which was in part why I saw things differently. When I returned to the United States, the only teaching position I could find on such short notice was with the University of Maryland's Asian Division, which sent professors to American military bases in the Far East. I would be teaching writing courses for American servicemen and servicewomen and their families, part of a program enabling them to receive bachelor's degrees from the University of Maryland while they were still with the military. In January 1987, I found myself living on Kadena Air Base in Okinawa, Japan, along with a dozen or so other University of Maryland teachers and thousands of American service personnel. In March, Mamoun arrived in Japan with all his worldly possessions in a backpack and an engagement ring in his pocket. Three weeks later we were married at the city hall in Naha, Okinawa, a totally emotional decision that I have never regretted for a second.

Because teaching positions were still scarce in the United States, I either had to continue with my University of Maryland position in Japan or go back to Saudi Arabia, where King Saud University had just begun a graduate program for women students. I liked my University of Maryland students, and the life of a "logistically supported scholar," as we were termed, wasn't bad at all. My students were adults who wanted to learn what I could teach them; their travels and the mix of people they had known had made them friendlier and far more sophisticated than almost all the students and most of the professors I had known in the States. My colleagues were a hard-

123

drinking (the tax-free booze in the BX and the itinerant life may have had something to do with this) but interesting group, mostly teachers who were dedicated, adventurous, and well-read, but who had lacked the luck and/or guile to get themselves tenured. And if I stayed with the Asian Division, I would travel to other areas of Japan and possibly South Korea. I would have led a different life and perhaps become a different person if I had stayed. But I couldn't resist the call of the Arab world or the lure of teaching graduate students.

Saudi Arabia had changed as much as I had in those four years. Riyadh, a work in progress when I left it, was now a gleaming modern city with an L.A.-style highway system, dozens of luxury hotels, and parks with trees and grass where families picnicked; many of the souks were now replaced with shopping malls; the old city still lurked behind the new one, but I saw it most in the shops and restaurants that were run by and catered to the "guest workers" from Egypt, Lebanon, Yemen, Syria, Jordan, and Palestine.

The university also was outwardly more attractive. The women's college had moved from the bleak collection of walled buildings that made it feel like a convent to a sprawling, parklike campus with a grove of palm trees in the center and flowering vines concealing the outside wall. The students, I was told, had also changed; fewer were daughters of foreign Arabs or of Saudi families rumored to have controversial political views. But I found them as lively, thoughtful, and articulate as before, if perhaps a little more wary about discussing their private dissatisfactions with their foreign teachers.

Some of the people I had known before were still there too. I had kept in touch with Zainab, and our friendship continued as before. The only difference was that her two daughters were now in college back in Egypt. Rasheed, the Palestinian boy I had met during my first weeks in Saudi Arabia, was now working in a pastry shop. He had never finished college, in part because he had spent more time socializing than studying, in part because his parents had lost most of their money. I learned then for the first time that Palestinians and other foreigners were not allowed to own businesses in Saudi Arabia. Instead, the business had to be placed under the name of a Saudi sponsor, who officially owned the operation even if had invested no money in it. At any time, the Saudi partner could claim the business for himself. And this was exactly what had happened to Rasheed's father, who was now living in Jordan in very reduced circumstances. (It was what happened later to hundreds of thousands of Yemenis, who were declared personae non grata during the Gulf War.) It was this bitter experience, and his own sense of failure, I think, that had made Rasheed turn to political Islam, as he had, most fervently. There was no discussing ideas with him now. He had The Answer. I thought of the bright, cheerful boy I had known and what he could have become had he had rights and a country—and yet, I suppose he was better off than most Palestinian men his age. In fact, the Saudis had almost recruited him to fight for Islam in Afghanistan, and if he hadn't changed his mind at the last moment, he would have become one of those desperate "Afghan" *mujahadeen* now excluded and persecuted as potential subversives by almost every Arab regime.

Things like that made politics matter to me now in a way it never had before. And if the world I had known when I first lived in Saudi Arabia had been almost exclusively feminine, middle-to upper-class, and bilingual, Mamoun introduced me to a much broader range of society, as well as a political world of which I had been largely un-aware. Between finishing his master's and starting his Ph.D., Mamoun spent a year in Riyadh, free-lancing his literary work to various Saudi magazines, gathering information for his Ph.D. dissertation, getting to know some of Riyadh's writers and editors, and chatting in cafés with poor Saudis and Arab guest workers who told him tales of exploitation and abuse few Westerners would have had the chance to hear.

I myself made different sorts of friendships than before. I now became friends with an American woman who had married an upper-class Saudi and was finishing a master's degree in Middle East studies. She told me what to read to fill in the gaps in my knowledge of Middle Eastern history and culture. I also met some Saudis who had lived for a long time in the United States and who had made their own comparisons, drawn their own conclusions, and formed their own criticisms of the two societies. I met a trilingual (Arabic, English, and Greek) Cypriot electrical engineer who acted as the Greek embassy's translator when Greek foreign service personnel went to visit their own and other expatriates in Saudi prisons, and an Englishman who taught Saudi Air Force cadets. This was at least a vicarious contact with a Saudi world outside that of the well-brought-up young ladies of the women's college. And if I did not agree with all that these men and women said, at least I had the benefit of hearing about what they had seen and listening to their knowledgeable and carefully consid-ered interpretations of the worlds through which they had moved.

16

Lies and Libraries

Sitting across from me in the men's library was a woman I had never seen before. Once a week, the men's library, a palatial seven-story glass and steel building with holdings in English as good as most university libraries in the United States, was open to women professors and graduate students. The regular male librarians left, the librarians from the women's campus took over, and no men were allowed in the building. At the back entrance to the library (the front entrance was closed), a male guard checked the ID cards of all the women as they signed in and out. Senior undergraduates could also come, but they could not check out books, and other women undergraduates were stuck with the useless library at the women's campus. These elaborate precautions, I was told, were designed to prevent men disguised as veiled women sneaking into the library to meet women, although why anyone would sneak into the library to meet a woman when he could see her far more easily in a shopping center or supermarket was beyond me.

My Saudi office partner had a different explanation of the precautions. "It's really to keep the women students from thinking," she told me. "Although," she went on, gesturing at the stack of freshman compositions she had just marked, "to look at my first set of papers, I don't think there's much threat of that."

Whatever their purpose, the regulations, combined with the distance of the men's library from the women's campus, greatly limited the number of female library users. ESL teachers, mostly British, came to check out novels, Arab women from the medical and social sciences departments came to do research, as did some seniors and graduate students from the English department, and I came to browse through the scholarly journals in British and American literature, although the subscriptions to most of them had run out in 1986, along with the oil boom. I also had to be there to help my students find the books they needed, because I had discovered that if I didn't take them by the hand and show them these books on the shelf, they would swear that no such books existed. (I couldn't blame them too much for this, however, because they'd never been taught how to use a library, and the librarians weren't much help because they didn't normally work in that library and were not familiar with its English-language holdings.)

I had come to know most of my fellow library users by sight, but the woman across the table from me was an enigma. For one thing, this pretty green-eyed blond was checking out books in Arabic. For another, I knew that she wasn't in the English department, and she didn't look like the women from the ESL department, who tended to be dowdy and middle-aged. She also had an *abayah* and scarf folded neatly on top of her purse, a clue that she wasn't Western. I knew some Syrians were blond, but they usually also had aquiline noses and prominent cheekbones. This woman looked Scandinavian. The mystery only deepened when she asked me for a pen in accentless American English.

"Do you teach here?" I said.

"Um, no." she said. "Actually, I'm not exactly supposed to be here, but they decided to let me use the library as a courtesy while I'm working on my thesis."

Talking to her, I learned that she was getting an M.A. from Harvard (she lowered her voice when she said it, shy about seeming to show off) in Middle East studies. She was writing about medieval Arab maritime technology, hence the Arabic books she was checking out. The topic sounded respectably dull, especially to someone like me, who didn't even know that there was a medieval Arab maritime technology.

"Neither do a lot of other people," she told me. "Arab traders were sailing all the way from Aden to China six hundred years before the Spanish and Portuguese started out on the open sea, and yet everybody in the West has the idea that the Arabs were just sort of wandering around in the desert living in tents all that time. And they think it's just some kind of coincidence that the Portuguese and Spanish got all these sailing urges immediately after they drove the Muslims off the Iberian peninsula."

Clearly this was a topic on which she had impassioned opinions.

"And they think it couldn't have anything to do with learning Arab trade routes and sailing techniques," she went on, and then checked herself. "Don't get me started on this. I'll go into a rampage about it and you'll think I'm some kind of nut."

Well, I did think she might be some kind of nut, but she seemed to be a more interesting variety than the teachers at the college who devoted their creative energies to making up gossip about one another. We exchanged names (hers was Barbara) and phone numbers. "By the way," I wanted to know, "what are you doing here? Do you have some kind of research grant?" I thought of the American graduate students I had known in Egypt, but somehow she didn't seem like them, even on this first meeting. She seemed both too beautiful and too angry to be the kind of person to get a research grant, publish a book, and move on to a tenured position at a good university.

"Oh, no," she said, getting up and wrapping her scarf and *abayah* around her. "I live here. My husband is Saudi. I've lived here for about eight years now." A dark-skinned woman who was also wearing an *abayah* appeared, to whom Barbara spoke in Arabic. The woman picked up Barbara's books.

"It amazes me when Americans can learn Arabic," I told her.

"It amazes me too," she said, as we started down the corridor toward the back entrance and the parking lot. "I wish I were one of them. I mean," she said, gesturing at the books her maid was carrying, "I can read it all right. I have to look up words a lot, but I can follow it because its classical Arabic, which is what I was taught." She was walking and talking so fast that I could hardly keep up. "But when I talk I make a lot of mistakes and I mix the classical and the colloquial Arabic together in a way that native speakers think is the most amusing damn thing they ever heard. The person carrying the books snickers at me every time I speak. Oh, here we are."

She and the maid disappeared into a shiny black Jaguar, and I, now standing alone in the afternoon heat, tried to figure out which one of the waiting taxis was the one I had come in.

It wasn't until several weeks later, when my boredom had enlarged enough to overcome my shyness, that I finally decided to call Barbara. An English-speaking maid answered, informing me that the princess would be with me shortly.

"Are you a princess?" I asked as soon as she came on.

"Has that goofy girl been answering the phone that way again? I just hate that. It sounds so pretentious. And it's not exactly accurate either, but let's not get into all that."

Instead, we got into Middle Eastern history. In college, I had taken several good classes in Western European history (although they had been called things like "The History of Civilization"), and I had assumed, until I went to China, that I had a basic grasp of the world's major historical events. Then I had learned that Han Dynasty China was every bit as artistically, philosophically, and technologically advanced as classical Greece, as well as much larger, and that T'ang Dynasty China, not the Holy Roman Empire, was the most developed society of medieval times. This led me to believe that there might be certain gaps in my knowledge of Middle Eastern history as well, and I wanted to know what to do about it.

"Start with Philip Hitti's *History of the Arabs*," Barbara told me. "It was written back in the thirties but its been updated since then and it's a good basic outline. In fact, I can lend you my copy."

And it went on from there. Hitti's book was informative and easy to read. I had previously thought it odd, for instance, that within a couple of dozen years, Islam had gone from being a group of believers in an out-of-the-way city in western Arabia to the cohesive force behind an empire that stretched from Baghdad to Alexandria and later from India to Spain. How could most of the Byzantine Empire, the heirs of the Romans, have fallen to a small group of horseman with swords? Because that was not the way it had happened, Hitti told me. Nor, according to Hitti, did the Muslims burn the library at Alexandria. As for the stereotype of Arab backwardness that my fellow expatriates were so fond of, as Hitti put it, the Abbasid courtiers were debating Aristotle while Charlemagne's lords were learning how to write their own names. Given Hitti's credentials (he was a professor of Semitic languages at Princeton and his book is considered a classic in its field), it seemed unlikely that he was some isolated lunatic making all this up, but I still thought it was wise to look at other sources. They concurred. My knowledge of history had just been turned upside down.

I was not entirely surprised that I hadn't been taught any of this before. The discrepancy between popular Western impressions and what authorities in Middle Eastern history had documented through their research seemed like a modified version of what one of my Chinese colleagues had called the "rascals and bandits" theory of history. This theory was not his own, he hastened to explain, but was in fact the invention of a bitterly ironic Han Dynasty scholar, and ran something like this: Whenever a challenge to the rulers of the empire prevailed, it was because the rulers had become corrupt and lost the mandate of heaven, and the challengers were the worthy heirs to their authority. The mandate of heaven was now rightfully theirs. This was known, of course, because the scholars of the new rulers were the ones who wrote the history books. If the challengers lost, on the other hand, it was because they were rascals and bandits who did not deserve to rule, again because it was the rulers' scholars who recorded history. Today, postmodernist thinkers have advanced similar theories, apparently unaware that the Chinese had the jump on them two thousand years ago. However, as phrases, I prefer "rascals and bandits" to "delegitimizing the narrative of the Other," and besides, it always brings back to me the gentle and ironic voice of my Chinese colleague.

Sometime in the eighteenth century, I reflected, the Arab world lost whatever challenge it had previously posed to the European empire and thus had gone down as history's rascals and bandits. Of course, Hitti's book and others like it were in almost every university library, where the intellectually curious could get a different view of world history than the one presented in the mass media and European history textbooks. Historians like Hitti, however, were seldom taught in undergraduate survey courses, where most educated people formed their sense of which people accomplished what in the history of the world.

And how much does a book in a library do? I couldn't help noting that my *Houghton-Mifflin World Almanac*, in its headline history of the world, still listed as fact the Arab destruction of the library at Alexandria. Later that year, I saw two casual references to the Arab destruction of the Alexandria library in book reviews in the *New York Times*. It wasn't even presented as a debatable theory. It was as if Hitti had never written. Rascals and bandits.

I thought about this often in the ensuing years, this relationship between lies and libraries. In most of the Arab world, the press is censored, and in the West, it is governed by market forces that frequently find it expedient to ignore the experiences of the poor, the powerless, and the foreign. University libraries are not censored even in Saudi Arabia and are less governed by market forces. A good library lets everyone know that the world is not simple, that there are many versions of events and many interpretations of ideas. It gives people a chance to learn things other than what their society wants them to know. It lets them know when they are being lied to, when they are being told half-truths and oversimplifications, when their emotions are being manipulated to suit ends that they would find morally repugnant. I suppose that's why it's so easy to believe that other people would burn them. But there is a corollary to this. The authorities do not need to burn a library if few people have the intellectual curiosity to want to use it.

In the Riyadh library were scholarly books giving a variety of Israeli, American, and Palestinian views of the Arab-Israeli conflict, for instance—from Jewish critics of Israeli human rights abuses, from Zionists, from policy analysts, from American Mennonite and American Friends Service Committee relief workers in Gaza. From such an American writer, I learned for the first time that in 1946, more than 85 percent of the land in what is now Israel had been owned by Arabs. If my students had read these books, I reflected, they would not have been so quick to tell me what Americans and Israelis thought and felt and knew, as if they all thought the same thing. And yet my students could not read those books, because most of them were not allowed in the library. And since the books were in English, probably only senior and graduate English majors would have been able to read them anyway. These students were usually too busy researching their senior projects and graduate theses in the literature section to give much thought to current political history.

Perhaps this compartmentalization of knowledge worked as well as any censorship to keep readers away from books, I reflected later, when I was back in the United States. The same books about the Arab world that I found in the Riyadh library were in Southern Illinois University's library too. And from the checkout dates stamped inside the back covers, I gathered that they were equally unread.

I thought about this compartmentalization of knowledge again a few weeks later, as Barbara and I stood in the archaeology section of the library. It was strange to realize that although I had now lived and taught in four different countries, I had seldom ventured out of the 800s (the literature section in the Dewey decimal notation) of any library. Like most academics, my approach to knowledge had been more like a farmer's than a mariner's, more like the old Yankee farmer in Frost's "Mending Wall," who knows his own field and says "good fences make good neighbors." The poetic alternative to Frost, I came to feel, was Tennyson's Ulysses, who says he will "follow knowledge like a sinking star / beyond the utmost bounds of human thought." I suppose this is what educators might call the interdisciplinary approach, but it has always been faintly suspect.

Thus I stood amazed and a bit aghast as Barbara sailed around the library, taking books from the art section (to look at bas reliefs that showed the riggings of Greek and Roman ships), from the architecture section (to find out if there was a difference between Arab and Roman building techniques), from the medieval European history section (to see what the medieval European monks had to say about their encounters with the Saracens), and from the Chinese history section (to find accounts of how Chinese and Arab technologies had interacted). All the while, she expounded upon her theory to me. The Arabs, not the Chinese, had invented the compass and gunpowder. The Arabs had trading outposts all through southern and central Europe until the time of the Crusades, which, she would have me know, were about trade, not religion. And in fact, the Arabs had discovered America. Well, actually, probably, the Phoenicians discovered it first, but anyone who lived on the Iberian peninsula could reach the Caribbean in a month or so, just sitting in a raft. Besides, thirteenth-century writers from Muslim Spain knew the world was round and reported claims that Arab mariners had circumnavigated the world, and the early Portuguese and Spanish explorers had Moorisko (Arab Christian) navigators. If the Phoenicians could get from Lebanon to Spain, they could get from Spain to the Caribbean. If the Arabs could get from Aden to Guangzhou, they could get from Portugal to Florida. She took Thor Heyerdahl's *Early Man and the Oceans* off the shelf and thrust it into my hands.

"Here," she said. "Read this."

All of this was interesting if a bit dizzying. The unconventional scholars that Barbara admired (Immanuel Velikovski and Barry Fell, as well as Heyerdahl) had arresting theories that had grown out of knowing more than one academic discipline, and if their theories were as yet unproven, they seemed well argued and thought-provoking. And Barbara's own theories were not as farfetched as they sounded at first.

Apparently, her committee at Harvard did not think they were wholly improbably either, because they passed her thesis, and I later found references (in Basil Davidson's *Lost Cities of Africa*) to the Moorish writers and navigators of whom she had spoken. She thought the Arabs might have invented gunpowder because she assumed that like the Greeks and Romans before them, the Arabs had built on existing technologies—in this case, Byzantine weaponry such as flame throwers and Greek fire. She had also found a record of saltpeter's being mined in Iraq in the ninth century. What would anyone be mining saltpeter for except to make gunpowder, she wanted to know.

"To sell to the Chinese to make firecrackers?" I suggested.

She ignored me. At the very least, she argued, it was the Arabs who had first used gunpowder as a weapon, because she had found a crusader's account of a battle in which the writer spoke of the Saracens pointing their flame throwers to the skies. "You don't do that with a flame thrower," she pointed out to me. "You do that with a propelled missile that has a trajectory, like a primitive cannon ball. And this was before Roger Bacon had written down the first European formula for gunpowder."

Okay. It sounded a bit like Russian revisionist history to me, or like the theory I had heard advanced (and that Nigerian writer Wole Soyinka had mocked so amusingly in one of his essays) that Shakespeare was really an Arab (Sheik Zubair). What some people took as an academic joke had been taken quite literally by the less well educated, and I had many bootless arguments about the theory with Arab friends who knew nothing about British literary history but assured me that England was too culturally backward in the sixteenth century to have produced a cosmopolitan and learned man like Shakespeare. They didn't know what to say when I asked them if Christopher Marlowe and Thomas More had been Arabs too.

But about Barbara's theories, I was not in a position to argue. I only knew the conventional wisdom, and, as Heyerdahl had observed, if one accepted the conventional wisdom that Stone Age people could not travel across thousands of miles of open ocean, then it logically followed that all of the Pacific Islands were uninhabited: the Tahitians had never reached Hawaii, or the Maori, New Zealand. And yet there they were.

Barbara thought the Arabs had invented the compass because "compass" was an Italianized version of an Arabic word, *boosalla*, something that turns on a pin. She discounted the common idea that the word came from Latin, claiming that the problem with European medievalists was that they didn't know Arabic and so couldn't recognize Arabic words and concepts when they saw them. Besides, she declared, Arab traders were sailing to China and the East Indies. The fact that the first compass had been found in China rather than the Middle East did not deter her, either. "Who needs a compass?" she asked me. "People who are sailing up and down rivers or people who are sailing across thousands of miles of open ocean? It's just easier to find things on land. The early Arab compasses are probably on wrecks at the bottom of the ocean, so nobody has found them yet." (Actually, according to what I read later, she was wrong about the Chinese, who did have ocean-going ships and probably sailed as far as the east coast of Africa. But her theory may still have been valid.)

I also read about the Kingdom of Saba (in what is now Yemen) and the excavations in Bahrain and theories about the origins of the Indo-Europeans (in a *Scientific American* article) and the customs of the ancient Celts. I had sailed away from the 800s to a New Found Land, but I did not quite know what to do with it. It had changed the way I thought about world history and civilization, about what early peoples had accomplished, about the ways in which they were both the same as twentieth-century Westerners and different from us. That was the most valuable knowledge, to know that people as intelligent and sophisticated as we are experienced the world in an entirely different way. But to me, it still seemed like a vacation from the real world of academically respectable scholarship, in which American literature experts argued about whether the textual evidence of Emily Dickinson's poems suggested that she was preoccupied with food (an actual article). Perhaps this is part of the reason that the Chinese used gunpowder only for fireworks and the Incas used the wheel only on toys. To use the knowledge for anything other than a mental holiday was too much of a threat to the established order.

Still, it was Barbara and the King Saud University library and the leisure to read that my work at the university gave me that enabled me to find out about all these wonderful and curious facts and theories and ideas. Perhaps, I thought, thousands of years from now, some archaeologist would find that beautifully constructed library, and perhaps the dry air of the desert would have preserved most of the books long after the acres of Western newsprint has moldered away. Then a different version of twentieth-century history would emerge from the one we think we are experiencing now. The archaeologists would find the hulks of the BMWs and Mercedes that the Saudis had imported and assume they were made locally; they would find the American-designed highway system and all the airfields and military equipment put in by the U.S. military for the Gulf War and think they were Saudi technology. Riyadh, the conventional wisdom would run, was obviously the century's center of learning and technology as well as being a great military kingdom that could summon vassals from thousands of miles away in North America to fight their wars for them. This would be especially likely if the mandate of heaven had shifted back again to the Middle East, and Westerners had become history's rascals and bandits. I wondered how many intellectual mariners would be around to question this version of history.

17

Maids and Slaves

The young woman came into my office, flustered and out of breath, to explain why she had missed class that morning. Her maid had escaped, she reported, and so there had been no one but she to stay with the children. If I had given an unannounced quiz, could she please make it up?

The woman had always struck me as very pleasant. She was always polite and attentive in class, and she worked hard at rewriting her compositions to improve her English. All this made me assume at first that the problem was linguistic.

"You mean your maid quit," I told her. "If you say she escaped, it sounds as if she were a slave."

"No, she escaped," the woman insisted. "These worthless Filipinas are like that. We pay their tickets to bring them here to work, and then if every little thing doesn't suit them, they run away and stay in their country's embassy, and we have a terrible time getting them back."

Yes, I guess "escaped" had been the right word, I learned later. The maid was not exactly a slave. After all, she hadn't been captured and brought to Saudi Arabia against her will. She was paid a wage, at least in theory, and supposedly she would receive a ticket home when her contract expired. But she was not free to leave, even if she could pay her own way home. In fact, she probably was not even free to leave her employer's house, because employers often failed to issue domestic workers the *iqaama* (work permit) without which all foreigners in Saudi Arabia are subject to arrest. Because her employer was required by law to keep her passport, she would have no way of proving her identity if questioned by the police. (The university had my passport, too, but I had an *iqaama* and the university was far more likely to return my passport if I wanted to leave.) There was no official agency to which she could complain if the terms of her contract were not met, if she were physically abused, if her employers failed to pay her, or if they refused to return her passport to her and give her the agreed-upon ticket home when her contract expired. She was totally at her employer's mercy, a fact she may not have known when she signed the contract in her own country. So if she was not exactly a slave, the fact that she could be unpaid, locked up, and beaten seemed to make the distinction technical.

When I was teaching in Saudi Arabia the first time, I had heard of a few incidents of abuse, but I had not paid much attention to them because I hadn't realized how prevalent the problem was. And I'm afraid, like many other Westerners, I didn't think of these Third World domestic workers as being like me; their possible mistreatment did not seem a matter of grave concern. It was the same sort of attitude, I think, that later led Western journalists to focus on the problems of wealthy, educated, English-speaking Saudi women and ignore the far more serious plight of the Third World "guest workers." It is easier to deplore the fact that an educated professional woman would be obliged to wear an *abayah* and would not be allowed to drive a car than to worry about a poor Sri Lankan woman's being beaten.

Nevertheless, one story I had heard then did move and disturb me. Fayruz, who worked for a friend of mine, was a young Eritrean woman who had been sexually assaulted be her previous employer. I didn't know whether she had actually been raped, or if her employer was just a sort of Saudi Bob Packwood, but I guessed she had been raped or threatened into having sex with the man, from the hushed tones in which my friend discussed it. I had seen Fayruz, a very lovely, fragile-looking woman of about twenty. Perhaps it was seeing her that made me sympathetic. Here was a real person who said good morning to me and brought the coffee whenever I visited, a woman as graceful and well-mannered as the young ladies who sat in my classes every day.

Fayruz and her sister had come to Saudi Arabia to escape the civil war in Eritrea. They were grateful to get jobs that would allow them to support themselves and their remaining family. But work in Saudi Arabia was not what they expected; although the sister's employer was a decent person, Fayruz's took advantage of the fact that she was virtually his prisoner to press his attentions upon her. Only the unusual fact that she had a sister nearby (and perhaps also that she was a Muslim) saved her. When Fayruz's employer started making advances at her whenever his wife was away, she called her sister.

Fortunately, Fayruz's sister was employed by a pious Saudi man who was disgusted that a man would abuse a servant that way. Outraged, he told the abuser that he would tell other people about the harassment if Fayruz did receive permission (required by law) to transfer her work permit to another family. Fearing the scandal and social ostracism that would result from such a rumor, the abuser agreed. And that was how Fayruz had come to work for my friend, who treated her as the contract had specified.

Her story, I think, is illustrative in many ways. Luckily, through an act of kindness, she had escaped her employer's continued sexual predatation. Unluckily, because she had no practical legal recourse, her employer went unpunished. The problem is not that Saudis are likelier than anyone else to sexually abuse their women employees (the numbers of women harassed by their employers here in America should quash that idea). The problem is that Saudi Arabia has no labor laws to protect the employee. About the only protection that does exist is the law that bars single men from hiring women servants and the fact that most Saudi wives would gather up their children and go home to their parents if they thought their husbands were sleeping with their maids. Obviously, however, this is not enough, or stories like Fayruz's would not happen. Worse, a Saudi employer could conceivably threaten a woman with arrest for prostitution if she refused his advances. A friend of mine, who acted as a translator for Greek embassy officials visiting prisons, told me of women prisoners who claimed that they were in prison for that very reason. Perhaps they were lying to appeal to my friend's sympathies; perhaps they were telling the truth.

What I learned on my own concerned minor physical abuse (mostly slapping and hair pulling, mostly done by the employer's wife), and great financial exploitation. I was told about it by employers and employees alike during my second visit. I think I heard more about it the second time in part because during my first years in Saudi Arabia, more of my students had been foreign Arabs who couldn't afford servants. I also think that being married to an Egyptian had made me more sympathetic to the foreign poor. And the situation itself may have gotten worse. The cleaning staff at King Saud University, for instance, was not being paid, at least according to the cleaning women who talked to me about it, hoping I could do something. Most of the women were Sri Lankans, recruited by a Sri Lankan company, which supposedly paid them. But apparently some middleman was pocketing their wages. Because they weren't allowed to leave the university compound, there was nothing they could do.

The situation of privately employed housemaids was much the same. In their essays and in the spoken English class, many of my students expressed the belief that it was entirely proper for maids to be confined to the house at all times, even though their contracts allowed them a certain number of days off.

"If you let them out, they'll prostitute themselves," several students explained. "That's what those Filipinas are like." Nor did they think it was unfair to ignore the parts of their maids' contracts that required the employer to allow the maid to return home once a year for a vacation.

"They'll just run away, and then you have to go through the process of looking for a maid all over again," one woman told me, a sentiment echoed by many Westerners with maids.

Westerners also, like some of the Saudis I knew, would lend out their servants as if they were slaves. One woman routinely sent her maid to clean the house of a friend who didn't have a maid, and neither thought to reimburse the woman for the additional work. Even Barbara surprised me one time by giving me a skirt her seamstress had made.

"Shouldn't I pay this woman for her time?" I wanted to know.

"Why should you?" she replied. "She gets paid whether she works or not, so why shouldn't she make a skirt for you?"

I still feel guilty about not insisting, and yet, it was so much easier to just go along with it. And worse things than this happened. Some of my students felt justified in slapping their maids.

"I know it isn't nice," one girl said, in a spoken English class debate about servants, "but if they won't obey you, what else can you do?"

Another girl, however, objected to this as un-Islamic. "It says in the Qur'an that you should treat a slave kindly. Isn't a servant entitled to as good treatment as a slave?" Unfortunately, this Islamic view does not have the force of law, despite the fact that Saudi Arabia claims that the Qur'an is its constitution.

The plights of the housemaids, and indeed of many other women workers, was complicated by stereotypes about their sexual morals that made many Saudi women fear and despise them and some Saudi men see them as fair game. Many Saudis I talked to (and some Westerners as well) assumed that all Asian women were prostitutes. For one thing, many upper-class Saudis had playboy relatives who had taken sex tours of Bangkok and Manila and inferred from the prostitutes they met that this was the normal behavior of Asian women. This notion, unfortunately, was not limited to the uneducated newly rich. Several of my colleagues wondered aloud how I could teach in China, where the women had no morals, apparently with no concept that there might be a difference between sexual habits of college students in the People's Republic and bar girls in Hong Kong. After a while, I became so annoyed with this attitude that I would point out that Western soldiers who had been stationed in North Africa during World War II had exactly the same opinion of the morals of Arab women, for exactly the same reasons.

The stereotype fit conveniently with the common Saudi notion that, left unveiled and unguarded, women would become sexually promiscuous, and, of course, it provided Saudi employers with an excuse to keep these foreign women locked up, no matter what their contracts specified. At any rate, partly as a result of the stereotyping and partly as a result of the laws that put all the power in the hands of the employers, Asian housemaids' complaints about sexual abuse tended to be ignored, and their running away attributed to lack of sexual opportunities rather than violation of contract or physical abuse.

Muslim housemaids from Eritrea, Sudan, and Pakistan faired a little better, but not much. For one thing, many Saudis assumed that a Muslim woman who was willing to travel alone to another country without the protection of her family must have committed some immoral act. That these women might have lost their families during civil wars (Sudan and Eritrea) or natural disasters (Bangladesh) or that women in an Islamic society could lose their families' protection through no fault of their own (for example, divorced or widowed women who had no brothers willing to take them in) was not generally considered. Rumors abounded that Eritrean women had traded sex for passage out of their country, and many of the Arab women to whom I spoke assumed that once a woman had "fallen," there was nothing to prevent her from embarking on a life of prostitution. Moreover, if the maid was young and attractive, she posed a threat to the employer's wife in another way. The husband might conceivably take the maid as a second wife. From my composition students, I received themes describing how maids flirted with the husbands, "pretending to be sweet and gentle," while refusing to do work properly for the wives.

How much of this was perception and how much of it was actuality I don't know, but it certainly made some Saudi women feel justified in abusing the maid. Jealousy, after all, doesn't need much foundation.

Sometimes this had its comic aspect. One of my students, Fareeda, and her husband and children had gone on a skiing holiday in Switzerland, taking their Sudanese maid with them to look after the children. As they stepped out of the plane into the sub-zero temperatures, they suddenly realized that the maid didn't have a winter coat. So Fareeda's husband took the woman to a medium-price department store (whatever the Swiss version of Sears might be) and told her to pick out a coat she liked.

Fareeda was furious. "He's never taken me to a store and told me to pick out anything I liked," she fumed to me, weeks after the fact. "And besides, she picked out a dreadful silver and red and purple thing that made her look like a *sharmoota* [whore]."

I wondered when, since biblical times, a coat of many colors had been the focus of such contention. And how a coat designed for winter in Switzerland could make anyone look like a whore escapes me still. Nevertheless, Fareeda certainly felt that she should have picked out the coat and made sure it was suitably drab. This incident did not engender kindly feelings between the maid and the lady of the house. Her husband was forgiven; the maid was not. I didn't know whether to laugh or be shocked. But if a pleasant and attractive woman like Fareeda could get so worked up about a coat, I couldn't help wondering what less secure women might do. After all, there was nothing to stop them.

Another incident still haunts me. On the maid's evening off, the two-year-old son of one of my students drowned in the swimming pool. Her husband blamed the nursemaid for not being there; if she had been there doing her job, it would not have happened. He could have blamed his teenage nieces and nephews, who were supposed to be keeping an eye on the child, and he could have blamed himself, for not having the foresight to put a fence around the pool. And perhaps on some level he did, but those were not the feelings upon which he acted. When the maid came back, he punched her in the face, and he would have beaten her to a pulp if his brothers hadn't finally intervened. As it was, she had a black eye, a bloody nose, and a great many bruises. Of course, it is hard to criticize the actions of someone beside himself with grief and shock. The point is that the maid, as the outsider, was the immediate scapegoat, and there was no law to prevent him from beating her if he wanted to.

There are more than enough people to feel sorry for here: the little boy, dead before he had a chance to understand what it meant to be alive; my student, so devastated by her loss that she didn't return to school for months; even her husband, who had transformed all his grief into rage.

But for some reason, I felt most sorry for the maid, who must have cared about the little boy too. Perhaps I felt this way because it was too painful to imagine that mother's feelings when she saw her child's dead body pulled out of the pool; perhaps it was because the maid seemed so utterly alone. I could imagine her coming home happy and excited from her party, where she had been chatting and drinking Coke and listening to music with other women from her country, having as good a time with them as Westerners did with mixed company and alcohol. Then she would have walked into chaos and rage—the husband cursing her and hitting her, the wife sobbing, the drowned little body. At first, she wouldn't even have understood what was happening, and then she would have understood all too well.

Quickly, one of the husband's brothers had transferred her to his house, so the husband couldn't attack her again. Yet he too blamed her to some degree; he just didn't think she should be beaten. After all, she was a foreigner and everyone else was family. But later, as she finished out her contract at the brother's house, did she come to blame herself as well? In a way, that seems to me almost worse than the beating.

Maids are not the only people mistreated and exploited in Saudi Arabia. They are simply the most vulnerable. Arab men working in the Gulf states are also exploited and subjected to arbitrary arrest. Omar, a Palestinian cook at a sandwich shop that Mamoun and I used to go to, had paid several thousand dollars for a work permit for Saudi Arabia. Given the wage specified in the contract, he could pay back the cost of his permit in a couple of years (his family had gone into debt to help him obtain the permit) and then have enough money to support his wife and children. For this first six months or so, his Saudi employer did pay him the specified wage. Then, when the construction boom in Saudi Arabia tapered off and fewer foreign workers in Riyadh wanted inexpensive restaurant meals, his employer cut his wages. Finally, Omar was receiving only room and board, no wages at all. There was nothing he could do about it. He couldn't quit, because his employer had his passport and refused to transfer his work permit. When he complained, he was arrested as Shi'ite agitator.

"Omar a Shi'ite agitator!" Mamoun exclaimed to me. "This man doesn't even know the difference between Sunni and Shi'a." He was only released when his employer agreed to vouch for him.

His case was not unusual. Saudi friends of mine who owned a small business also cut the wages of their employees when business was bad. "It's the same as you would do in the States or Britain," the wife explained to me. "When times are bad, employees sometimes have to take a salary cut." Perhaps, but not in violation of an existing contract. And anywhere but the Gulf, the employee would have the right to quit if he didn't like the idea. And his union might decide to strike. In Saudi Arabia labor unions are illegal. And the irony is that there are poor Saudis who could take these jobs, especially the people called *fouqra' al-Haram* (the poor of the holy places), people born in Saudi Arabia who are the descendants of foreign Muslims who came for the Haj and stayed. However, as one Saudi man pointed out to me, "They wouldn't work for what we pay them, and the foreigners are easier to control." Indeed, if they were treated like the foreign workers, they would quit and go home; the foreigners can't.

Of course, many Saudis do not mistreat their employees and some object to the laws that permit unscrupulous people to cheat and beat so easily. The problem is that there is little that they can do about their feelings except try to help out in individual cases, as the employer of Fayruz's sister did. There is absolutely nothing they can do publicly without risking arrest. The journalists and editors I met through Mamoun had been threatened with arrest for even the mildest criticisms of Saudi society. A Saudi writer we knew, who had made the alarming suggestion that schoolgirls would be safer in traffic if they were not required to wear face veils, was told he would be fired if he wrote more radical pieces like that one. His predecessor had been fired and blacklisted, and had had his passport taken away from him for similar sorts of criticism. Another writer, Fawzia al Bakr, who submitted an article more comprehensively critical of the situation of women, was jailed for three months. Later, in 1993, a group of Saudi clerics were arrested for founding a human rights organization.

This made me all the more irritated that most American journalists did not write about this massive exploitation of Third World people, which was right there before their eyes. They could have exposed what was going on without any danger to themselves. During the Gulf War, Saudi Arabia was full of Western journalists who, unable to say much about the war itself, wrote about everything from dinner parties to shuwarmah sandwiches to veils, everything except the situation of the foreign workers. It was as though half the population of Saudi Arabia (actually, foreign workers are probably slightly more than half the population) had become invisible.

It struck me as ironic that while Bush was declaring that it was immoral for any country to keep foreign workers who wanted to leave (meaning, of course, the Westerners in Iraq), no one seemed to notice those millions of Asian and other foreign workers in Saudi Arabia and wonder if they were free to leave. I could understand how the reporters might mistake all the foreign Arabs for Saudis, but did they really think all those Koreans and Filipinos and Pakistanis were Saudi citizens there in a war zone of their own free will?

18

Outside and Inside

For me, Saudi Arabia, despite its vastness, was a country of interiors.
The world I lived in was behind the walls of houses and apartments,
inside cars, and behind the walls of the women's campus. Even the
trips outside walls were to areas carefully defined in time and space—
to the fenced-in "family" park a few blocks away, to the shopping
streets, to the bookstore.

To be outside any of those carefully defined limits was to feel in
danger in a way that I seldom had the first time I was in Saudi Arabia
and never did in Egypt. Now, cars followed me at a crawl when I went
down the empty side streets to the grocery store just a few blocks
away, and if I wanted to walk to Zainab's, who now lived about a
quarter of a mile away on University Street, a main thoroughfare, men
would yell vulgarities at me out of car windows. This was very different from the *"ya helwa"* mashers of Cairo. Their being in cars while I
was on foot made it frightening, as did the fact that the streets outside
the main shopping areas were almost deserted. Although I don't think
I was ever in any real danger, I felt intimidated. The atmosphere was
claustrophobic, and even though I grew used to it, that accommoda-
tion in itself began to change me.

I was intimidated enough by the changed atmosphere to start
wearing an *abayah,* for instance. For one thing, even Western women
who ventured outside normally wore *abayahs* now, and I began to feel
a little like an exhibitionist without one. For another, the university
had recently asked that all the women professors wear them to and
from work, "Especially," the chairwoman explained, "those of you
who are relatively young and relatively slim, and might attract male
attention." Of course, this appeal to female vanity worked when
threats and pleas would have failed. None of the female faculty would
admit to being relatively old, relatively fat, and incapable of attracting

male attention, particularly in relation to the other women in the department. We all started wearing *abayahs* to work. As a garment of female incapacitation and propriety, the *abayah* is not as uncomfortable as the pantie girdles into which American women squeezed themselves in the early 1960s, but I still didn't like it much. It took one hand and an elbow to keep it closed, making it impossible to carry a sack of groceries or anything else other than a small purse, and because an *abayah* had armholes rather than real sleeves, it ripped if you reached for anything. All you could do in it was stand around with your arms at your sides. And being swathed in black did not make crossing streets at night any safer. (I remember once looking around unsuccessfully for reflector tape such as joggers sometimes use and pet owners put on dog collars.)

Nor did all this veiling accomplish its intended goal. If it was supposed to be a sort of portable wall, as I understand it is in some countries, it didn't work. A woman on foot, accompanied or unaccompanied, was a target. The veiling only worked as a sort of back-up signal, if she were already inside a car or a building. One evening, when Mamoun and I were walking home from Zainab's apartment, I was made aware of how the veil didn't help, and also of what the constant sense of vulnerability was doing to us both. The street was almost deserted, just a solitary car or two on a four-lane highway. The houses were all hidden behind twelve-foot privacy walls of beige brick; even the balconies of the apartment buildings faced the side streets, so that from the main street the buildings looked uninhabited.

Because the sidewalk was so narrow that we could walk only in single file, I was walking a little ahead of Mamoun. Suddenly, a little Sri Lankan man pulled into the parking place beside where I was walking, hopped out of his truck, and then, apparently on a sudden inspiration, barred my way and smacked his lips at me as I tried to walk by. I don't know what had got into him. Most of the Sri Lankans I had met seemed like gentle, polite people, and the man would probably have never acted that way in his own country. I also can't see how I could have been much of a temptation. In my *abayah* and headscarf, I looked about as provocative as a bag of laundry. But he seemed to think he had spotted someone more helpless than he was—a woman alone—and decided to take advantage of the situation. Apparently it had never occurred to him that the man walking a few paces behind the Western woman could have any connection to her. (Why would the woman be walking in front, after all?) I was about to wallop the little creep with my purse when Mamoun realized what was going on and lunged for him.

It was gratifying to see the man's expression change from lewd self-assurance to panic and watch him take off running. Motivated by sheer terror, he dashed across the street and into the building where he worked, a little store that looked to be the only inhabited edifice on the street.

Realizing that he couldn't catch the guy, Mamoun threw his shoe at him instead. This is the ultimate insult, next to spitting at someone, and the man had definitely made sure that he was not within spitting distance. Even the shoe, which caught him in the back, didn't slow him down. But there was now a problem; Mamoun was standing in the middle of the street with one shoe on and his other shoe on the opposite sidewalk. At the time, it didn't seem as amusing as it does in retrospect.

Fortunately, the manager of the store, an Egyptian, had been watching the whole episode. Coming out and picking up the shoe, he crossed the street, handed it back, apologized for his employee, and invited us for a cup of tea. The incident was beginning to turn into something like the Cairo street disputes where strangers intervened and calmed the combatants down. But he also had a certain vested interest. He definitely tried his best to convince Mamoun over a cup of tea that it would not be a good idea to call the *mutawaeen*, the morality police.

There was good reason to want to avoid the *mutawaeen*. They had the power to arrest anyone (except, of course, the royal family and their multitudinous in-laws) for any behavior an individual *mutawa* considered un-Islamic. With no written laws, no one in Saudi Arabia can know what is considered legal and what is not, or what the punishment might be. Saudi Arabia claims its constitution is the Qur'an.

As for the case at hand, the Qur'an, as far as I know, gives no specific punishment for making lascivious faces at women, but it's pretty clear that you aren't supposed to do it. The *mutawa* could have done whatever he chose with the man. Because there were no public trials and no adversarial legal system in Saudi Arabia, a *mutawa*'s accusation was tantamount to a conviction. So it was not surprising that the Egyptian manager of a little appliance store didn't want anything to do with the *mutawaeen*.

"You could always bring the little squirt out here and let me take a swing at him," I suggested as a compromise, but the manager was not about to let either of us set eyes on the miscreant again. Later, thinking more calmly, both Mamoun and I realized that this was more of a cuss-him-out offense than a wring-his-neck offense, but at the time, the Sri Lankan bore the accumulated weight of a year and a half of similar behavior from people safely ensconced in cars, where we couldn't get our hands on them.

I think incidents like this explain why being out of doors came to feel like something dangerous and forbidden. Even Mamoun was vulnerable. On several occasions, he was stopped by *mutawaeen* who wanted to see his identity papers and scolded him for not being in the mosque during prayer time or for wearing a T-shirt depicting the pagan shrines of ancient Egypt.

"Why is it," I asked Mamoun when we had both calmed down somewhat and had resumed our walk back from Zainab's, "that when you don't want a *mutawa,* they're all over the place, but there's never one around when you need him?"

But, as I said, there were also outdoor interiors, where we were no longer as vulnerable. The same distance in the opposite direction would have brought us to the family park, deserted by day, except sometimes in the winter, but at night filled with Sudanese and Egyptian picnickers, sometimes families, sometimes groups of women. (Saudi families seemed to do their picnicking in the desert because they knew the terrain well enough to drive off the main roads without getting lost.) Not only was it cooler at night, but at night women could slip off their headscarves and loosen their *abayahs* without anyone noticing. Clusters of adults ignored the benches and sat on the grass, laughing and talking, while older children kicked soccer balls around and smaller children slept with their heads on their mothers' laps. Arab families didn't seem to separate adults and children as Westerners often do: here children and adults alike took long afternoon naps, and children often stayed up late in the evening, probably because it was only after dark that children could play out-of-doors without risking sunstroke. I don't know if the parks ever closed, but sometimes, passing by at eleven or so, we would see parents tenderly placing sleeping children in the back seats of their cars.

This, I thought, was what a city park should be. There wasn't much to it, really: not many flowers, a great many panhandling cats, and a fountain that we could sometimes hear beneath the murmur of voices. But the sky was always cloudless and starry, the grass was cool, and the peacefulness made the park seem far away from the rude drivers and officious morality police that made the rest of the city so frightening.

I also felt relatively comfortable on the main shopping streets a few blocks further on, where women's clothing and jewelry were sold, because this meant that there would be a lot of other women around. Still, I was often stared at, and because Mamoun could understand the muttered comments our appearance together elicited, there was a certain tension. When I was alone or with other women, I was all right, perhaps because I couldn't understand what men were saying about me. It was our being together that was a problem. Mamoun was usually dressed in jeans and a T-shirt and I was obviously not Arab, so Saudi men tended to assume that he must be a some strange-looking Westerner too and felt free to discuss us in Arabic—whether we were actually married, for instance, or whether I might become equally interested in one of them. Mamoun, in turn, went around muttering things like, "For staring like that, may God grant that you go cross-eyed and never again see anything but your own ugly nose." In this well-lit and crowded public place, the hostility was unlikely to transcend the verbal, which I thought rather remarkable considering the colorfulness of the words exchanged. Perhaps this is one of the benefits of a highly verbal culture.

The most civilized place within walking distance was the big bookstore that sold magazines and newspapers from all over the world, where the clientele was more interested in browsing through books than in staring at women. Even Saudi women flipped up their face veils to scan the newspaper articles. Walking through its automatic doors (the only set of them I had seen there except at the big international hotels) into the air conditioning was almost like walking from Saudi Arabia into a college bookstore in the United States. They carried textbooks, volumes on how to pass the TOEFL (Test of English as a Foreign Language) and GRE, classic novels, British detective stories (to which both expats and English-speaking Saudis were addicted), art supplies, reading lamps—the only items missing were sweatshirts and beer mugs. They made up for this deficiency by having a rack of French novels, mostly by Georges Simenon. They also had books in Arabic, although most of them were translations of European novels. Novels by Arab writers were too likely to be controversial.

The Riyadh bookstore was a bookstore in which one could browse. Because the foreign newspapers and magazines were expensive (about ten dollars, for instance, for an international *Newsweek*, and a dollar for the Egyptian *al-Ahram*, which sold for fifteen piasters in Cairo), Ma-moun and I would catch up on the news by standing by the display reading entire articles. No one ever asked us to buy or leave, nor were there any pointed notices informing us that this was not a library. People reading were special people.

And people who wrote were even more special. When the Saudi managers found out that we were both publishing in local (and in Mamoun's case, Egyptian) magazines, they became downright defer-ential, calling us Doctor (accent on the second syllable) and Doctora, putting aside for us copies of the magazines with our articles in them, and generally treating us with the exaggerated but rather gratifying respect we normally received only from Arab students.

It was strange to me, this respect for the written word and those who produced it, together with the banning of books and the persecu-tion of writers. But of course, on another level, it makes perfect sense. Autocratic governments only need to ban books if people pay any attention to what writers think. And although the bookstore, as I said, seemed like an American college bookstore and a place of relative safety and freedom, it was indeed only relative. Sometimes whole issues of foreign newspapers and magazines were not allowed into the country; this meant they contained articles critical of Saudi Arabia. More often, the censors carefully inked out critical sentences in news articles, along with the bare arms and legs of women.

I couldn't help wondering, sometimes, about the relationship be-tween the black ink covering controversial sentences and paragraphs in news articles, the black ink covering Maggie Thatcher's legs, and the black *abayah* covering me as I stood there trying to read. Did this mean that in Saudi Arabia, you could see the news as long as the news was wearing an *abayah*? Or did it mean that they felt that free political thought was as tempting as exposed female flesh? It interested me later that the American reporters covering the Gulf War made a great fuss about the *abayahs* covering women but scarcely mentioned the veils over the printed word. A different sense of what was important, I suppose.

There was another paradox about the bookstore and Saudi censor-ship. Aside from Saudi Arabia and female flesh, one could learn a great deal more about the world in this store than in most American bookstores. They carried English-language newspapers from around the world: the *London Times* and the *Times of India*, as well as Nigerian, Philippine, and Japanese newspapers. When American television announcers later described Saudi Arabia as being "isolated" and "out of touch with the world," I wished I could ask them how many Americans knew there was a civil war going on in Sri Lanka or that the government of Sudan had collapsed. In Saudi Arabia, it was easy to know these things. What you did not know was who within the country had been arrested, who had disappeared, who had had a prince intercede for him and been freed, guilty or innocent. You did not know if the people executed as common criminals were really criminals or if they were political dissidents. Indeed, you never read of any crimes at all, much less of trials. You did not know about the behavior of the royal family. You did not know about attempted coups, or the defection of Saudi diplomats. In short, Saudis could not legally read anything that might make them think badly of their government. But, as they did know their news was censored, people of normal intelligence usually thought badly of the government anyway. They just didn't know that things were any better any place else. This nationalistic sentiment was confirmed by all the bad news they read about the West in Saudi newspapers, which was every bit as misrepresentative and sensationalistically reported as American news coverage of the Middle East. If the veil didn't work very well, the make-up did.

It also interested me that in Saudi Arabia, there were more enclaves for exposed flesh than exposed news. In the compounds of foreign companies, in the diplomatic quarters, and in the international hotels, women wore Western clothes with little fear of harassment from strangers or arrest by the *mutawaeen*. These were placed reserved for the rich and the foreign, however. The people who needed to be intimidated, the Saudi middle class and the Third World workers, were excluded either by custom (middle-class Saudis) or by price (everybody else).

And even the "Western enclaves" were still only outdoor interiors, places where, temporarily, the rules did not apply but were always subject to the possibility that this special dispensation might be revoked. Sometimes the morality police did raid the parks, or the international restaurants, or the foreign compounds, or even the homes of foreign diplomats. The safety of these places was illusory, just as the safety supposedly provided by the veil was illusory.

Still, it was something. Accurate news was a great deal more difficult to find. Even the *Voice of America* and the *BBC World Service* shortwave broadcasts contained very little news unfavorable to the Saudi kingdom. To get uncensored news about Saudi Arabia, you had to leave the country, and even then the sources were questionable. Arab newspapers tended to have their own party lines and regime censorship to deal with, and American papers often printed "See how awful the Arabs are" articles that indicted the Saudi people rather than their government. Saudi dissident scholars who published outside the country were almost the only reliable source.

Nevertheless, most foreigners and many Saudis in Saudi Arabia were too busy worrying about their own safety to consider the larger political picture. Although one could forget the immediate danger some of the time, ordinary people going about their daily business were always vulnerable—especially, but not exclusively, women. Both the street harassers and the *mutawaeen* saw to this, almost as if they were acting in concert. My Cypriot friend was once detained and interrogated by the *mutawaeen* for ten hours. He had been wearing a cross around his neck, and when a *mutawa* had demanded that he remove it, he had argued in Arabic that the Qur'an taught that Christians and other people of the book be allowed to practice their religion without interference. At this point they arrested him. As the interrogation progressed, he began to fear that they didn't believe that a Christian Cypriot could speak Arabic and quote the Qur'an. They thought he was an Arab Muslim who had converted to Christianity. Apostasy, he knew, carries the death penalty in Saudi Arabia. He remained convinced that if the *mutawaeen* had not called his employer, finally, to verify his identity, he would have been killed.

Nor did following the laws, or what people thought were the laws, make one safe. After all, you can't know what the law is if it isn't written down anywhere. Supposedly, Muslim women were obliged to cover their hair but not their faces. There is a specific Hadith that says that the parts of a woman's body that can be shown in public are her face, hands, and feet. And supposedly, women can hire taxis or ride in cars with men other than their husbands or fathers if the man is clearly a paid driver, and if the woman is sitting in the back seat.

Zainab knew an Egyptian taxi driver who would drive her wherever she needed at a discount price; he was honest and reliable, but the drawback to this arrangement was that he was given to tiresome and childish practical jokes. (He liked to lock the automatic doors just before we tried to get out of the car, for instance, and then laugh at our frustration.) One time, when she had asked him to drive her to a bakery to order a cake for her daughter's birthday party, he insisted on taking her to another bakery instead, where he assured her she would get a better price. She insisted on her original bakery. He drove her to the one he wanted to take her to, laughing because the doctora couldn't do anything about it; they were laughing and arguing when he pulled up in front of the bakery, and she refused to get out, saying that she was on strike until he took her to "her" bakery. Ignoring her protests, he went in to order the cake anyway. While she was sitting in the car, a man began peering at her and signaling for her to roll down her window. She ignored him. But when the driver returned, the harasser announced that he was a *mutawa*, demanded to see their identity cards, and told them that he had seen them laughing and joking together in an obviously immoral way. And what decent woman went around with her face uncovered? He demanded that she cover her face, or they would both be arrested. Terrified, she complied.

"What could I do?" she told me. "He could have arrested me as a prostitute. I could have ended up in jail for the rest of my life."

When I later told the story to a Saudi friend over a cup of tea, she sighed but seemed unsurprised. "Those *mutawaeen* are so corrupt. He was probably angry that she wouldn't flirt with him and decided to scare her. It's terrible what those people can get away with." The Saudi woman herself was safe from the *mutawaeen*, but that was because of her family connections, not her nationality.

Saudi women were certainly not safe from harassment. Veiled from head to foot, a Saudi colleague of mine, having worked later than usual, was standing by herself outside the college gates waiting for her husband to drive her home when foreign workmen at a nearby construction site started yelling obscenities and throwing bottles at her. Plastic bottles, it is true—but it was the thought that counted. I could imagine her standing there next to the high, dun-colored wall that surrounded the campus. The street would now be empty of most of the cars that crowded around the gate when classes finished, just a solitary car every five minutes or so, with staring men who might circle back again just to see if she might be available. Nothing else but dust and heat and silence and a few bits of paper blowing down the street in the hot desert wind. Should she go back inside and try to call a taxi? But then she might miss her husband, who might be angry at having driven all the way to the college for nothing. And then the insults, the bottles, the panic.

"I don't know whether they were trying to make me yell at them, so they could tell from my voice if I were old or young, or if they just saw a Saudi woman standing alone and decided to use me to show how much they hated Saudi Arabia," she told me. When her husband finally arrived, apologizing that car trouble had delayed him, she burst into tears as soon as she got in the car and cried all the way home.

Of course, an incident like this could happen to a Western woman in a Western city too, especially if she were of a different ethnic group than her tormenters, as was the case with the Saudi professor. But in a Western city, the woman would probably have been driving to and from work herself, and not have to wait outside. And in a Western city, a woman would usually know what areas to avoid. In Riyadh, it could happen anywhere, any time a woman happened to be alone, however briefly. The whole out-of-doors was an area to avoid, and the police were more of a danger to ordinary people than criminals were. I came to think that what made Saudi Arabia so dangerous was not the physical threat (after all, no one was actually hurt in any of the incidents that I knew of), but that the constant fear so often turned into hate, a hatred fed by isolation and misunderstanding, dividing people along ethnic and cultural lines.

The Western expats tended to assume that the Saudis were themselves exempt from harassment and arrest, and that they approved of the mistreatment of others. Many thought that absolute monarchy was a Saudi tradition and that the persecution of non-Muslims was endorsed by Islam. Oblivious to the treatment of the Third World guest workers, the Westerners were also sure that they themselves were the chief targets of the *mutawaeen*, because Western ways were more antagonistic to Saudi tradition than the customs of the TWNs (this stands for "Third World National" in the same sense that "wog" once stood for "worthy Oriental gentleman"). And at least, if the nonacademic Americans I sometimes met at parties were any indicator, they tended to think that all Arabs were the same. They assumed that the few foreign Arabs they could identify as such held the same values they ascribed to the Saudis, and blamed Saudi xenophobia for the unpleasantness of midlevel bureaucrats who were sometimes foreign Arabs with their own grudges against Westerners.

The fear and the sense of victimization certainly could do terrible things to Americans. In 1988, I was at a Fourth of July picnic given by the American embassy when the news came over the loudspeaker that a U.S. navy ship had just shot down an Iranian commercial airliner, killing everyone on board. Many of my fellow American expatriates clapped and cheered. Could they all have been that way before they came to Saudi Arabia? I think the racism of the American expats bothered me more than any of the other forms of racism I encountered, perhaps because I had somehow expected better of Americans.

There was certainly enough anger and resentment to around. I didn't know any Asian workers well enough to know how they felt, but the foreign Arabs I knew were sure that Westerners were better paid than they were for doing exactly the same work and that Westerners were much less likely to harassed or arrested by the *mutawaeen* than they were. (The former, at least, was true. Although Zainab and I had received our Ph.D.s at the same time and had the same years of teaching experience, I was getting a higher salary because I came from a "developed country.") The foreign Arabs I talked to also resented the Saudis even more than they did the Westerners, because they felt that Saudi traditions were being imposed on them as Islam, when their own more liberal interpretations of Islam were far more valid.

As for the Saudis, some of the professional people I talked to felt that foreigners were given preferential treatment for jobs because foreigners could be fired more easily; and as one Saudi man told me, "The government doesn't need to share power with its citizens as long as it can hire foreigners to do all the work. Why should the government hire a Saudi who might have controversial views or come from a tribe who once opposed the Sauds when they can so easily hire a foreigner who'll do whatever he's told?" So in essence, many of the foreign workers were scab labor, although they didn't know it.

Some of these same Saudis also told me that the Saud regime was virtually controlled by the U.S. government. The Saud regime got to keep the oil profits from territories to which it had only the most dubious claim (the oil reserves are primarily in the Shia region, not the Saud family's traditional domain, the Najd) and the American military trained the secret police that kept the regime in power. In return, the Saud regime kept oil prices down and bought millions of dollars worth of unneeded American weapons. It sounds too simplistic, and yet I have read this as well. And it also partly explains another curious fact. The husband of one of my upper-class Saudi students had received military training at Fort Benning, Georgia; I recall that I thought at the time that it was odd that he would have to go all the way to the United States to learn how to fly a plane. Later, I read that Fort Benning had become notorious for training Central American military officers later involved in human rights abuses, so notorious, in fact, that after the U.N. report on the Salvadoran death squads was released, there was congressional debate about discontinuing the program. Was that what my friend's husband was really doing at Fort Benning?

At any rate the result of all this rumor and suspicion was that people who could have had common interests tended to blame one another, each thinking the other group was getting special privileges while their own group was being singled out for harassment. In a way, all this fear and anger and scapegoating were in the regime's interests, because all the misguided resentment prevented any concerted effort to expose the regime's exploitative practices and human rights abuses. At paranoid moments, I was sure that this was the *mutawaeen's* real function. I thought all too often of the lines from Auden:

> Intellectual disgrace
> Stares from every human face
> And the seas of pity lie
> Locked and frozen in each eye.*

And at such times, I began to wonder if Saudi Arabia in the 1980s were not a microcosm for the ethnic and cultural hatreds later to cleave the world apart in the Gulf War: the divisions were the same—the rich Arabs, the Westerners, the poor Arabs, and the rest of the Third World. It was as much to avoid such paranoid moments as it was to avoid harassment that I resigned myself to living behind walls as much as I could. And on one level, at least, the walls worked. Within the walls of my apartment, I entertained friends from Saudi Arabia, Palestine, Britain, Egypt, and Cyprus, none of whom I would have met if I hadn't come to Saudi Arabia that first time. Within the walls of the campus and the library, I encountered ideas I would never have understood or appreciated if I had stayed at home. And within the walls of the park and the bookstore, there was even the reassuring presence of non-threatening strangers. I was happy enough and, I thought, relatively unscathed by living in a country where no one had any rights. Happy within limits.

* From "In Memory of W. B. Yeats."

19

Passage

I was standing in front of the class in my bare feet, as it was so hot that even my sandals were sweaty. Besides, taking off one's shoes indoors was far less unconventional in Saudi Arabia than it would have been in the States, and I liked to indulge myself. Part of my mind was on whether to turn on the air conditioner, which would eliminate the sweaty foot problem as well as the physical discomfort of my students. On the other hand, it would force me to bellow to make myself heard over its roar, making me hoarse by the end of the day. The rest of my mind was on the clash of cultures in *A Passage to India* and what my students had to say about it.

The novel is too beautiful and complex to summarize easily. The plot concerns several intelligent English people's responses to India under British rule, and a strange episode, never explained, in which an earnest and broad-minded young Englishwoman, Adela Quested, believes that Aziz, her Indian host on an excursion to the Marabar Caves, has sexually assaulted her. She is not raped; she simply thinks that when she was alone in the cave, someone, whom she assumes is Aziz, lays hands on her in a way she interprets as sexual. Despite the fact that Aziz apparently had nothing to do with whatever happened, he is immediately jailed and tried on the basis of her accusation. Only one Englishman, Cyril Fielding, a free-thinking schoolteacher who had been on the brink of a friendship with Aziz, believes in his innocence. At the trial, Adela Quested realizes that she doesn't know exactly what happened, and she can't say for certain that her attacker was Aziz. She admits this, and Aziz is released, much to the disappointment of the British community. This episode only covers the first half of the novel, and even in this first half, the symbols of the cave, the heat, and the natural life of India suggest some kind of power at work that is beyond rational comprehension, something hostile to intrusion. The novel is an odd and oddly successful mixture of social and political realism and early modernist symbolism, with all that symbolism's complex philosophical and poetic implications. And the novel does not end with Aziz's acquittal, but goes on to examine the complex course of the friendship between Aziz and Fielding.

This clash of cultures was not new to my students. For one thing, like the Indian Muslims of seventy years ago that Forster depicts, these young women lived in a society where reputation was extremely important, where the actions of an individual reflected on his whole family, and where both social and family obligations were far more important than they are to most Westerners. They also knew, through their reading of literature and from the Westerners they had met, that most Western societies were somewhat different from this, although how much they knew about the differences and the assumptions behind them varied from person to person.

Salwa, the daughter of an Arab father and a British mother, knew these differences very well and had clearly been thinking about the comparative merits and disadvantages of two societies for some time. She had also experienced directly and repeatedly what many of the other students only sensed: the ways in which the racist assumptions of the British Raj—that the natives were too emotional and disorderly to be able to rule themselves, that they came from a backward and lethargic civilization, and that even the best of them could never be quite like us—permeate much of the current British and American thinking about the Middle East. Because Salwa looked and spoke like an Englishwoman, unsuspecting Brits and Americans had apparently held forth about the awfulness of Arabs in her company, little thinking that this well-spoken, well-educated, blue-eyed blond was an Arab herself.

I knew of other students in the class who had contact with the West as well. Amany, a pretty young Egyptian woman, had spend a summer working as a receptionist/desk clerk in a tourist hotel in Cairo, despite her parents' objection that such employment was not suitable to her social class. Fatma, a serious-looking Saudi woman whom I particularly liked, often entertained the wives of visiting American and British diplomats while their husbands discussed affairs of state. And there were also some Palestinian students in the class who saw parallels between the Israeli occupation and the British Raj. (I often wondered how they would have compared Forster to some of the liberal Israeli writers, like David Grossman, but unfortunately I

didn't get the chance to work with them after the class was over.) Of
the rest of the students, some had traveled to Europe on family vaca-
tions, but I didn't get to know them well enough to know what kinds
of experiences they had there. Nevertheless, the fairly small group of
English majors all knew each other, and they had certainly had the
opportunity to compare experiences among themselves.

When I started teaching the class, I was aware that Forster's well-
intentioned liberalism had certain limitations. It's hard not to notice
that although Forster has three major British characters, Cyril Fielding,
Mrs. Moore, and Adela Quested, all of whom enlarge their understanding of themselves as a result of their encounter with India, there
is only one major Indian character, Aziz, and he is a sociable, harmless
man who lacks the emotional and intellectual complexity of his British
counterparts. Moreover, he is merely embittered by his encounter with
the British, gaining no self-knowledge and becoming overeager to cate-
gorize and stereotype all British people until Fielding seeks him out in
an attempt to renew the friendship. I pointed this out to my students,
as well as some of the generalizations that Forster makes about "the
Oriental mind."

At one point, for instance, when Miss Quested has recanted her
attempted rape accusation and Fielding unsuccessfully tries to per-
suade Aziz to forgive her, Aziz makes unpleasant remarks about Adela
Quested's appearance; Fielding expresses his disgust with "the Oriental mind" that judges women solely according to their physical appearance, comparing them to motor cars if they are beautiful and maggots
if they are not. I suggested to my students that this might not be a
uniquely "Oriental" attitude, or Americans wouldn't have sayings
like, "She's so ugly I wouldn't take her to a dog fight even if I thought
she could win." Besides, Aziz had been quite willing to befriend Miss
Quested, plain or pretty, before she mistakenly accused him of sexual
assault.

Perhaps this made the students more willing to be frank about
their own responses, or perhaps it set them on a track they found
congenial anyway. At any rate, they were so excited by the approach
that I often had a hard time getting them to see Forster's fair-minded
insights and basic good intentions and returning them to the larger
philosophical points of the novel. They wanted to talk about the novel's politics; I wanted to talk about its philosophy. But the resulting tug
of war made the class one of the most exciting I have ever taught.

The Saudi woman, Fatma, had an intriguing question that set a whole line of other questions in motion. We were discussing the scene in which Fielding visits Aziz, finds him surrounded by his Indian friends, and joins in a general discussion of politics and religion in which he casually acknowledges that he is an atheist. All the Indians other than Aziz are shocked.

"I found his behavior rather confusing too," Fatma commented. "He talks to people he has just met about his private religious doubts when most people would only reveal something like that to their most trusted friends. And yet I've noticed Westerners will often do this sort of thing. Why is that?"

I tried to explain that I thought Fielding is trying to convey that he's a progressive, honest, open-minded person and that he does not have any religious prejudices against the Muslims. But it was more than that. Atheism itself meant something different in the West, and I didn't know how I was going to explain its lack of stigma. More complex still, I didn't see how I could explain to students living in a religious police state that among some Westerners, at least, discussing politics and religion could simply be a way of getting to know people. Finally, I told her that there were many Westerners who didn't give much thought to religion and felt that it was hypocritical to pretend they did. In fact, it was because they were ethical people that they were so ready to admit to being atheists, even though they might not have any carefully thought-out reasons.

In the Muslim world, or at least the part of it that I saw, it seemed to me to be much more difficult not to think about religion, especially if you rejected it. I also think that in much of the Muslim world as well as among devout Christians, many people assume that religion is the basis of morality. Dostoyevsky has written, after all, that if there is no God, then everything is permissible, and if one thinks deeply enough, I suppose this assumption is true. Yet since Fielding, after all, is an Englishman, not a Russian, it is simple enough for him to be an un-thinking but ethical atheist. Aziz and his friends, and indeed my students, on the other hand, had difficulty imagining such a world. To them, Fielding has just announced that he is a totally immoral person.

Fatma agreed with this analysis, and added. "I can see how he might say something like this to Aziz, who knows his real character. But in front of other people? What he has said would be embarrassing to Aziz, too. I'm surprised that Fielding could live for so long among Muslims and not understand this."

Later, I thought back over both the scene and the discussion. I though about it later that year when an American woman journalist interviewed a group of Saudi women professors and me about politics and religion and went away blandly assuming that the rigid official answers the Saudis gave her were their real feelings. But what I thought of more was Fatma's question about why an intelligent and well-meaning man like Fielding could make such a blunder. Finally I decided, with some surprise, that it could be because there is no real reason for Fielding to learn about what would disturb or embarrass an Indian Muslim; there is not any social penalty for shocking natives. The only people who matter to him socially are the other British, and with them he knows exactly how far he can go and still be tolerated.

Later in the semester, Fatma made another remark that caused me to wonder if perhaps the novel might have a political subtext that implied very different ideas from those normally attributed to Forster. Once again, we were talking about the relationship between Fielding and Aziz.

"One thing that puzzles me," Fatma said slowly, her pen poised over her notes, "is this. Aziz is a doctor, a very well-educated man, and Fielding is only a high school teacher. Yet Fielding treats Aziz like one of his pupils."

She was quite right. Fielding does treat Aziz like a pupil, at one point even lecturing Aziz about how he could improve his Urdu poetry, despite the fact that Fielding doesn't even know the language. And yet it doesn't seem jarring or presumptuous, at least to a Western reader, in part because Forster has depicted Aziz as a sort of adolescent. He is good at his job, but he has no control over his emotions. He mourns the anniversary of his wife's death one moment and plays polo the next. I explained that I thought this was a flaw in the novel, that all Forster's major British characters are intelligent and thoughtful although his one major Indian character is like a boy.

Her next comment took me by surprise. "Why is it," she said quietly, "that Western people feel that they're superior to everyone else?" There was nothing confrontational in her tone. She seemed genuinely puzzled about why we Westerners were beset by this odd illusion.

Of course, even most Westerners of Forster's time would have laughed at the theories he puts in the mouth of Colonel Turton, that all peoples born south of a certain latitude were emotionally unstable. And now, even the long-cherished idea that certain skin colors make you stupid seems blessedly to be on its way out. Unquestionably, however, Western people still do tend to feel superior to everybody else, the expats in Saudi Arabia being the example nearest at hand. At the time, I just said that I supposed that when Westerners came in contact with societies that were less advanced technologically, they tended to assume that the people from these societies must be less advanced mentally. The Westerners did not stop to realize that they were not personally responsible for the advanced state of Western technology, or that individual people from other cultures were not responsible for the political and social problems of their countries. That answer seemed to satisfy both her and the rest of the class, who had been listening very attentively for my reply. But the answer didn't satisfy me for very long.

When I arrived at the college at seven the next morning, I took a long walk around the campus and reflected on everything that had been said the day before. It was still cool then, and as I followed the gravel paths through the little groves of palm trees and across wide swatches of lawn dotted with flower beds, I thought over these questions and tried to find as many answers as I could. Of course, I considered the idea that if you haven't been taught another people's history and culture, they seem to you to be a people without a history or a culture, but this didn't seem to be a complete answer. It might apply to the Americans in Saudi Arabia, who could see only a transplanted Western architecture when they looked for culture and knew only a official sanitized version of the Saud family's early twentieth-century takeover of the Arabian peninsula for Arab history, if they knew any history of the country at all. But it could not apply to the British in India, who were surrounded by the monuments of a culture even older than their own. The answer to that sense of superiority lay elsewhere.

I came a little closer to understanding when we reached the closing pages of the novel. It had been difficult to explain to many of the students that despite all Fielding's broadmindedness and his rejection of the crude racism of the British military officers and other officials, he is still a firm believer in colonialism. They liked Fielding, and they wanted him to think as they did. And then, Fielding's proimperialist views established, I had a hard time convincing the students that Fielding was nevertheless intended to be a sympathetic character. In fact, I think Forster did well in not making Fielding a sort of patron saint of correct political thought, instead depicting him as a man of his time and place who just happens to be a little braver and a great deal more tolerant than the people around him.

Yet tolerance is very different from either understanding or respect, as Forster makes clear. At their final meeting, Fielding ridicules Aziz's idea of an independent India. It is in the midst of this argument that Aziz says,

> "Down with the English anyhow. . . . If I don't make you go, Ahmed will, Karem will, if it's fifty-five hundred years we shall get rid of you, yes, we shall drive every blasted Englishman into the sea, and then—" he rode against him, furiously "—and then," he concluded, half kissing him, "you and I shall be friends."
>
> "Why can't we be friends now?" said the other, holding him affectionately. "It's what I want. It's what you want."

As the heat of October faded into the almost bearable temperatures of November and the students switched from short-sleeved to long-sleeved blouses, we discussed at length why Aziz and Fielding could not be friends. Forster's answer, that the earth and the sky and horses didn't want it, is obviously a metaphor for a much more intangible obstacle. It felt too obvious and too glib to say that the obstacle is simply Aziz's anger and sense of injustice, or to suggest any Kipling-esque dictums about the incompatibility of East and West. What was it then? I looked out at the twenty faces looking back at me, some furrowed in thought, others hopefully waiting for me to tell them the answer. Finally, Salwa, the British-Arab woman, raised her hand.

"I think it's because friendship is a relationship between equals," she suggested. "You can have kindly feelings toward an inferior, but he can't be your friend. You can't be friends with someone you think is incompetent to run his own country."

A murmur of assent ran through the class; yes, this did sound right, although I later thought that I would have phrased it differently. The problem is that Aziz and Fielding are equals, but only Aziz knows this. Fielding doesn't even know that he doesn't view Aziz as an equal. It will take the loss of empire for even people like Fielding to realize what equality with a non-Western foreigner means. Most of us have a hard time realizing it even now. Power makes people feel superior to people who do not have power; otherwise, the powerful could not justify their power to themselves. I suppose this also partly answers the question of why Western people felt so superior, as I reflected the next day during my morning walk. And yet the novel isn't only about the blindness of power, but other kinds of blindness as well. The Marabar caves are in part an emblem of those blindnesses—the blindness of ignorance, the blindness of culture, the blindness of emotion—the list is all but infinite. And the same metaphor, I suppose, could apply to the attempts of my students and me to understand the novel. Their blindness was easy enough for me to see, especially when they were of the bash-the-British mode. It took me a little longer to realize my own. In discussing the scene when the British rally around the supposedly assaulted Miss Quested, condemning out of hand her supposed attacker, I asked the students if Forster was being ironic when he wrote, "Although Miss Quested had not made herself popular with the English, she brought out all that was fine in their characters."

"No," said Amany, the woman who had worked as a receptionist at a tourist hotel in Cairo. "He is not being ironic. That is the finest they can be—small-minded bigots." Apparently she had endured some tantrums from Western tourists who attributed imperfect hotel service and the general tribulations of travel to deficiencies in the Egyptian character. After overhearing one such outburst when I was in a hotel dining room in Cairo, I couldn't blame her for being fed up. But this wasn't Forster.

"Oh, come on now," I said, "I'm asking you what Forster thinks of the British, not what you think." But I did think she was right about Forster's not being ironic. He seems to me, I told her, to be pointing out that when people are acting their worst—in this case, assuming a man to be guilty, before any trial, of a crime that is totally out of character for him and that he has no motive for committing—they have often convinced themselves that they are doing something noble, in this case, protecting an Englishwoman's honor. They accept Miss Quested's confused account as fact, primarily because she is English, and do not even listen to Aziz's version of events, because he is Indian. In this hysterical atmosphere, they ostracize Fielding for even suggesting that Aziz might be innocent. And yet they can somehow reconcile this with their British concept of fair play, because they have extended the benefit of the doubt to Miss Quested despite the fact they deplore her taste in socializing with Indians. A less careful writer than Forster would have simply satirized them.

If Amany had been blind to some of Forster's subtlety, I had been equally blind to the growing implications of all those unanswered and interconnected questions. Why didn't Fielding understand what he was implying, why couldn't Aziz and Fielding be friends, why did Westerners feel so superior? Their questions made the novel a different book than I would have taught to American students. The book I would have taught, at least on the level of social realism, was about cultural misunderstandings and bad manners on the part of the British; what I read with my Arab students was a novel about the politics of domination. This came into clearer focus for me when we were discussing the British and Indian cultures by using the social anthropologists' concept of guilt and shame societies.

At the beginning of the novel, Aziz, a widower whose children are being raised by his dead wife's family, feels he cannot remarry because it would mean spending money on a new wife instead of on his children. To satisfy his sexual urges, he goes to prostitutes in a distant city where no one knows him, because it would mean public disgrace for both himself and his family if these visits became known. When he is accused of assaulting Adela Quested, the British authorities search his house and find letters he has has written to a brothel. They make the letters public, using them as evidence of Aziz's lechery. The shame brought on Aziz is not only the shame of the accusation, which his friends, at least, know is false, but the shame of having his private life made public.

I had often heard Muslims say that what you do in private is between you and God, but what you do in public is also between you and society. This had sounded like hypocrisy to me at first, until people pointed out that if you were a Muslim, you still believed that certain actions were wrong, even if you could not resist temptation. And having what is private made public is equivalent to having committed the sin in public. This is what happens when Aziz's letters to the brothel owner are revealed. Forster glosses over this a bit, but my students understood the significance of the revelation very well. The only equivalent in Western society, at least until twenty years ago, would have been revealing someone's homosexuality.

Amany, the girl who had worked at the hotel, had a question. "I can see that Aziz is shamed. He is arrested and jailed, he loses his reputation in the community, and the secrets of his personal life have been revealed to the public. I can see that Mrs. Moore seems to feel ashamed of the rude behavior of the British. But I don't see any 'guilt society.' What do the British feel guilty about?"

This was a good point, which was all I could say at the time. Later, it seemed to me that guilt does motivate the actions of both Fielding and Quested, after a fashion. Miss Quested recants her accusation, even though it brings her public disgrace among the British, because she would have felt guilty about sending a man to prison if she wasn't absolutely sure that he was the right person. Fielding makes himself a temporary outcast among the British by declaring his belief in Aziz's innocence, in part because he would have felt guilty if he had kept silent. But Amany was right; neither does feel guilty. In fact, they both feel somewhat pleased with themselves at having done the right things. And Miss Quested at least has reason to feel considerable guilt.

"So instead of talking about guilt and shame societies," Amany said, only half joking, "It might be more accurate to talk about shame societies and shameless societies."

Perhaps this lack of any sense of guilt doesn't bother Western readers as much as it did my students, I began to realize, because Forster only hints at the suffering that Miss Quested has inflicted. He has Aziz say, when he is arrested, "My children and my name!" but he doesn't show what this means, and immediately shifts the focus from Aziz's disgrace to the introspection of Fielding and Quested. The clues are there, but they are often clues only a person raised in a non-Western culture could interpret. And of what Aziz suffers in prison, we know nothing.

When Fielding and Aziz meet again at the end of the novel, Aziz is living in an autonomous Hindu princedom, supposedly to be as far away from the British as possible. His children are now living with him, as well as a woman to whom he is not legally married. His medical skills seem to have degenerated into a mixture of Western medicine and local folk medicine, which Fielding sees as proof that the Indians need the British to keep them modern. Aziz himself has become a rigid and bitter man.

It seems to a Western reader as if Aziz has degenerated, and that this degeneration bespeaks, somehow, a lack of character. My students had a very different interpretation. Fielding and Quested suffer temporary embarrassment and social ostracism from people they have known for a short time and do not like or respect anyway. Then they return to England and resume their normal lives. Aziz, my students pointed out, has been shamed in front of the community in which he has lived all his life. His disgrace and that of his family is permanent. Even though he has been acquitted of assaulting Miss Quested, his visits to prostitutes have become public knowledge. This exposure, my students suggested, is probably why his children are with him rather than their grandparents. His wife's parents could not subject themselves to the disgrace of raising the children of such a man. They can only hope that if their neighbors don't see Aziz and the children, their own connection to Aziz will be gradually forgotten. And why is he living with a woman not his wife?

"What family would marry their daughter to such a man?" a Saudi student wanted to know. The woman he is living with must be a social outcast like himself. Why indeed should he marry her? He no longer has any respectability to lose.

Seen this way, the novel changes radically. Aziz's bitterness, which seems so childish to Fielding, becomes totally understandable, and Fielding himself becomes annoyingly smug. Of course, the mores of Indian Muslims in the 1920s may have been somewhat different than those of Saudi Muslims in the 1980s—and yet I could find nothing in the text to contradict my students' inferences. And the larger inferences are even more disturbing. The Westerners feel no guilt because they have no idea of the consequences of the shame that they have inflicted, and there will never be anything to force this knowledge into their awareness. Forster lets his Western readers think the same way. Perhaps one way that power corrupts is by preserving a false sense of innocence.

"He should have made them know what they had done," Amany said.

I was not so sure. On the most obvious political level, the novel seems at first little more than a plea for a more benign colonialism. But those wonderfully ambiguous symbols of the cave and the mosque and the carefully observed details all say, "But there is so much more to it than that." Forster never tells us what this so much more is. Perhaps the evil within the caves is an evil that Mrs. Moore and Miss Quested brought with them—the evil of assuming a knowledge and power that is more than human. Perhaps its just as well that Forster never says anything like this directly. It's too harsh, too bare, too polemical. And it is as much because of the class as because of the novel that I continued to think about the book after I came home.

I thought again about shame societies and shameless societies when America celebrated its victory over Iraq. Nobody needed to read the reports about the massacre of a retreating army unable to signal surrender to the planes attacking it, or about the civilian casualties, or about the Iraqi soldiers buried alive in their trenches. And no one in America was obliged to see the continued suffering of Iraqi civilians under U.N. sanctions.

I thought, too, about the hysterical trial of Aziz before the trial of the men accused of bombing the World Trade Center, when politicians were fuming about lax immigration regulations for Arabs and the *New Yorker* ran a cover of an Arab child kicking down a sandcastle of New York. No one seemed willing to come forward and remind Americans that in our country, people are considered innocent until proven guilty. If there were such American versions of Fielding, they were not given any air time.

20

Sunset Cloud

It was time to leave Saudi Arabia, and again I was leaving for practical reasons. Mamoun had been accepted into a Ph.D. program at Southern Illinois University, and I had a good chance of getting a lectureship in the English department there. I had gone on the university's treasure hunt around the city getting all the signatures I needed for my exit visa, and I was now in the process of trying to pack two and one-half years of my life into two large suitcases. And yet I had only begun to learn about Saudi Arabia and the students I was teaching, and indeed about the politics and values of the world outside the United States. Going home was like moving back to a small town after living in a city. What should I take with me and what should I leave behind?

On a practical level, the sorting was fairly easy. I gave all my kitchen equipment to Zainab. She thought she didn't have any use for the coffee machine, until I explained to her that the instant "American coffee" she served to Western guests was every bit as bad as the Turkish coffee I tried to make. At this, she gasped and decided she could use the coffee maker after all. I gave away most of my long skirts, but kept the *gellabeyahs* for future use as lounging robes. I took my *abayah* and scarf, just for the sake of memory. And then there were my books and paintings and writings, all with memories attached to them, and the memories themselves. I kept worrying that I was going to forget something important.

Although my students had given me a farewell party, they still came individually to give me their addresses and say their own good-byes. They wanted to sit in my apartment, sip cups of tea, and be treated as friends rather than students. One girl wanted me to tell her fortune with my tarot cards. A very pretty girl from a wealthy family, she had several suitors, all of whom she liked "well enough." Just out of curiosity, she wanted to know which one she would marry. I gave a suitably ambiguous reading. (As it turned out, she later married another man altogether.)

Another student, Hind, showed me her witty drawings of Saudi life—a Saudi couple dressed for inside and outside the kingdom, for instance (*taub* and veil in one, tennis outfits in the other), and one of a peevish-looking, long-haired girl buried to the waist in a map of Saudi Arabia, with the caption "Stuck in the K.S.A." She signed the ones I liked best and gave them to me. While she was visiting, she admired a calligraphy scroll that an artist in Kaifeng had done for me when I was teaching in China, and I knew what that meant: it would be polite to offer it to her. But the scroll held memories for me—of my trip to Kaifeng with one of my students and her introducing me to the old artist in his studio. He did the scroll for me on the spot, looking at me a moment and then saying if I were Chinese, my name should be "sunset cloud"; then with huge, graceful strokes of the brush, he inked the words onto the rice paper. So at first I didn't offer to give Hind the scroll. And then, just after she left, I looked at the size of my suitcase and knew it was memories rather than objects I would be taking back. I ran to the balcony and saw her just as she was about to get in to her father's car. "Here, catch," I yelled, and I see still her surprised and happy face as she reached up and plucked the scroll out of the air.

Other students gave me other keepsakes—a silver bracelet, a book bag, a pendant, "So that you'll remember me," each of them said. And I did remember them. But I remembered words more than anything else, and for this I didn't need any keepsakes as reminders. I was reminded every time I thought of the books we read together.

The face and the words I remember most clearly were those of Almaz, a Palestinian woman graduate student with long, straight, black hair and high, broad cheekbones, who looked so much like a Native American that it made me realize, with a shock, how similar the fates of these two dissimilar peoples have been. I would see her there, sitting in my office, with her long skirt and her red satin blouse and all her gold jewelry—and I would remember that I had never seen her smile. I knew that she was very bright, very unhappy, and very drawn to fundamentalism, but I never understood how these three elements abided in her or shaped her vision of literature. I only knew that she said startling things. After we had read some American classics like *Winesburg, Ohio, My Antonia,* and *The Sound and the Fury,* as well as *Housekeeping,* a fine contemporary novel by Marilynne Robinson, Almaz had a question for me.

"In all of these books, people try to find their identities by leaving their families and communities and traditions. Quentin Compson commits suicide because he can't leave these things behind. Is this idea just in these books, or is this an American view?"

Of course, all of these writers make it clear that in leaving family and community behind, one also loses something, and Faulkner's most admirable characters tend to be people who stay in their communities but refuse to accept the injustice—people like Ike McCaslin and Lucius Priest, for instance. Yet I supposed that it was an American view that the community needed to be changed and that at least some of the community's values needed to be discarded. In fact, it was so much of an American view that I had never really thought of it as anything but a universal truth—that a person has to resist the false identities and values forced upon him by circumstances to find out what he really believes. It seemed as natural to me for George Willard to leave Winesburg, Ohio, as it was for a bird to fly the nest.

"But that's mad," Almaz blurted. "How can you know who you are without your family and your community? It is this that nurtures you, that protects your individuality from all the people in the world to whom you are nothing."

But I suppose you have to know you are nothing to most of the people in the world before you can feel that, and that sense is outside the experience of most Americans. And I also wondered if perhaps there was a difference in the community as well as a difference in the history that made us look at the world so differently. American writers wrote of communities that were quick to condemn unconventionality but slow to help people in need, where the tradition was to accept injustice to others (racism and class snobbery, for instance) and to respect success no matter how it was achieved. Those things had to be rebelled against, it seemed to me. Was the American reality truly so different from that of the Arab communities, or was it just point of view? Perhaps there are some ways of seeing that only being victimized can teach you, visions that can be gained only through loss.

I thought of this when Almaz and I talked about a Faulkner story that had always puzzled me somewhat, the title story from *Go Down, Moses*. In it Gavin Stevens, a well-meaning white lawyer, helps an elderly white woman, Miss Worsham, bring the body of her black servant's grandson home for burial. The man has been executed for murder, and Stevens had thought that the kindest thing to do was not to tell the grandmother, Molly Beauchamp, about the young man's death until months later. They could then just tell old Molly that her grandson had died, without telling her how he died. It would be too much shame for old Molly to bear, he thinks, if she knows her grandson was a murderer. Above all, he wants to keep it out of the local paper. He is astonished when Miss Worsham and Molly spend their last penny (and more—Stevens takes up a collection) on the funeral, and when Molly wants a notice in the paper. Stevens is left puzzling over the strange ways of black people, which he views with what seems like a kind of condescension. The story had always troubled me because it seemed to suggest that black people were so different from whites that even their grief was alien. At best, Molly's motive seems to be a blind love that denies her grandson any responsibility for his actions, and at worst, it seems like a childish love of display.

"I know why Molly wanted the funeral and the notice in the paper," Almaz said quietly. "She wants to show that her grandson was a man and not some piece of trash." I stared at her. It did sound right. And it would make "Go Down, Moses" a companion piece to another story in the collection, "Pantaloon in Black," in which a bigoted country sheriff misunderstands how a black man's grief over his wife's death has driven him into provoking a deadly fight with a white man. The sheriff concludes that black people have no natural feelings. And like the sheriff, Gavin Stevens, although he is a far more sympathetic character, still cannot know about what is not within his experience. Yet it is only the experience of the sufferer, and not the essence of the emotion, that is different.

I wondered how it was that Almaz could see this while I had missed it. I talked about it later with a Palestinian colleague.

"Because it's what the Israelis do to us," she told me. "When they kill men in prison, they won't give the bodies back to the families. They bury them at night, without prayers, where no one can know where they are."

I didn't want to ask her any more about how she knew this. It seemed too painful and too personal. And I later read the same thing. I don't think I could have begun to understand what this meant to the families, if I hadn't talked to these women and then seen the same experience reflected in Faulkner's Molly Beauchamp. I would not have understood that it was the ultimate gesture of contempt, a way of saying, "This man had no family, no childhood, no religion, no community, no hopes for the future, no chance of ever being any more than this. He wasn't a human being at all. He is just a carcass to be disposed of." And so Almaz knew why Molly wanted the body back and why Molly wanted a notice in the paper, and Gavin Stevens didn't know, and I didn't know. Faulkner knew, I think, and yet, like Forster, he allows the reader to avoid knowing.

That knowledge, those moments, were something worth taking back with me.

And I thought of another book, another face, another class. I thought of the shy Syrian girl, Amal, who wrote English badly and often stuttered when she spoke, and who thought and said things no one else in the class dared. I was teaching *A Tale of Two Cities,* focusing on both what Dickens said about prerevolutionary France and about the revolution itself. The love story, my students decided, was silly beyond words, and one student described Lucie Minot, Dickens's sweetly insipid heroine, as the most useless woman she had ever read about. "All she does is go around having long golden hair and fainting," she remarked. So we concentrated instead on Lucie's father, Dr. Minot, in solitary confinement for twenty years for having witnessed one of the crimes of the aristocracy, and on the story of the evil Marquis, who runs a poor child down with his carriage, throws the dead child's father a coin, and continues on his way. When the father follows the Marquis to his country estate and kills him, he is not only hanged for his crime, but the body is left to rot on the gallows as a warning to the other villagers.

"This all seems so barbaric and so brutal and so backward," I remarked. "American students often complain that these old nineteenth-century classics don't have anything to do with the world we live in today."

At this, Amal raised her hand. "You must be joking," she said. "There is no country in the Middle East where this wouldn't happen today, where it doesn't happen almost every day. Except that instead of leaving the murderer to hang, the government in my country might destroy the whole village." She may have been thinking of the destruction of Hama, a town in Syria that Hafiz al-Assad wiped out in order to eradicate the Muslim Brotherhood, but there were enough similar events elsewhere in the Middle East to make the students unsure exactly what country she was talking about. A gasp went through the class, and students in the front turned around to see who had said such a thing. Then there were whispers in Arabic, and the answer, "Suriya, Suriya." Amal was Syrian, not Saudi. The relief was all but visible.

She could just as easily have been talking about Saudi Arabia, and some of the students must have known this. A year or so later, back in the States, a Saudi student from the Hejaz told Mamoun that when he was a child, he remembered that "criminals" had been executed and their bodies left to rot. Then his older brother had recognized one of the corpses. It was one of his former classmates who had been handing out antiregime leaflets. His brother, the student said, had suffered from nightmares and nervous disorders ever since. He could only be thankful that he himself had been too young to understand what he had seen.

I didn't know the story at that time. It was only by bringing the memory of Amal back with me that I could piece it together with the Saudi student's story and reflect how unique the experience of most contemporary Americans is to so much of human history. At the time, I just weighed Dickens's reflections on the French revolution, its excesses and its inevitability, and wondered if the Arab world would experience a comparable revolution.

And we talked about Dickens's point that many of the French aristocrats escaped to England, leaving people like the marquis's faithful steward to bear the brunt of public fury. Again Amal raised her hand.

"The same is true now," she said. "The rich always find a way to escape while the ordinary people suffer. Right now Cyprus is full of rich Lebanese."

Well, that was not exactly what Dickens had said. It's easy to turn "some" to "all" and "sometimes" to "always." And yet Amal had given me different model, a different way of seeing, that would be one of the weightiest insights I would take back with me. In fact, I sometimes wished I could find some way of throwing this vision away, especially during the Gulf War.

Of course, I took back lighter things as well. I can't see a copy of Yeats's poems now without thinking of the time my modern poetry class diverted itself into a discussion of the romance between Yeats and Maude Gonne, the beautiful actress and revolutionary to whom he wrote so many of his love poems and who steadfastly refused to marry him.

"Why didn't she marry him?" a student who often spent most of the class admiring her manicure and whispering to the student next to her wanted to know. We had been reading "No Second Troy."

"Maybe he was ugly," the woman next to her suggested.

"His picture is on the cover of the book," I pointed out. "He doesn't look that bad to me."

Twenty young women flipped their books over to examine the photo on the cover, the one of Yeats as a young man wearing glasses and holding his mouth slightly open. Apparently, he was speaking when the picture was taken, but the effect is nevertheless not entirely flattering. Several of the students made dismissive tsks, the Arab equivalent of a thumbs-down gesture.

"I don't think he's ugly. It's just the picture that makes him look a little stupid," another student ventured. "And if any man was writing poems like that to me, I'd marry him in a second."

"No, she did the right thing," a visibly pregnant student pointed out. "It's better to marry a man who likes you than a man who worships you. To be turned into a statue to worship is not a good thing."

The unmarried students all wanted an explanation.

"A man who likes you will always like you. You can grow and change, and he'll feel sorry for you when you are sick," she explained. "But, *ya'ni* (I mean), who could keep thinking of a woman as Helen of Troy when she's pregnant and throwing up in the bathroom every morning."

So much for romanticism. I wonder now if some of my own baggage wasn't equally romantic.

These were some of the things I had tucked away in my mind. And yet I kept worrying about the things in my suitcase and fretting about what didn't fit. I had to leave my copy of F. O. Mathiessen's *American Renaissance*, which particularly pained me because I always look over what he has to say, and my own marginal notes, before I teach nineteenth-century American authors.

"I believe libraries in the United States do have this book," Zainab observed. "As long as you have your ticket and your passport, you don't have anything to worry about."

And maybe I did need to leave nineteenth-century America behind for a while. In fact, the only things I still have after four years are the images and the insights and the memories. They aren't any more suited to life in the United States than the veil and the *gellabeyahs*, and they have probably made me seem even more peculiar to the people I meet here. And yet I wish I had brought fewer things and more memories. My fear now is that I did leave something important behind. Some idea, some insight, something learned and then forgotten. It was hard enough to leave people behind, knowing I would never see what they would become. The people I knew are all frozen moments in time, images, statues. I heard a month or so ago that Hind, now twenty-five, has two-year-old twins. To me Hind is always a twenty-year-old girl, an immobile image of possibility and hope.

"Here, catch," I shout from the balcony, and Hind looks up, surprised, her hand up to catch the scroll forever in midair.

Contemporary Issues in the Middle East

Recent titles in the series include: